IT'S NOT ABOUT THE MONEY

HOW TO TAP INTO GOD-GIVEN GENEROSITY

TERRY T. MUNDAY

TQL
PRESS
Oklahoma City, Oklahoma

© Copyright 2009
Terry T. Munday
ISBN: 978-0-9824906-4-8
Printed in the United States of America
Cover Design: Wesley Hobbs
Graphic Design: Lyn Rayn

Published by TQL Press
P.O. Box 721243
Oklahoma City, OK 73172

TABLE *OF* CONTENTS

Every year I receive countless requests from fundraisers in need of donations. Amid them all, Terry Munday's initial request has stood out to me with his passion to maintain a worthy cause. Since that first meeting, I have worked with Terry on projects, and with each one, his understanding of fundraising's is evident to both his organization as well as contribution to God's plan for us. Now, Terry provides a refreshing look at the nexus of Christianity, giving, and business in *It's Not About The Money*. His expertise and sense of mission allow him to paint a true picture of fundraising and what it can really mean to God's vision for the world. Forget about going door-to-door — fundraising is so much better!

—David Green, founder and owner of Hobby Lobby

Terry Munday has been my pupil of sorts for many years. I have taken pride in encouraging him and watching his passion for fundraising mature. And as his fervor has grown, so has Indiana Wesleyan University. I'm thankful to have been involved in his work, whether it was telling him that I was always there for him if he needed guidance, or offering up my golf course year after year for his fundraising golf tournament. Like all of Terry's donors and supporters, the small things we do, the selfless acts of kindness that we express out of God's love for others, those are the things that make a difference to organizations in need as well as to God. That message rings clear in *It's Not About The Money*. Whether you are a Christian fundraiser or a potential donor for a not-for-profit, Terry's insight from two decades working as a fundraiser is rich in the humility, faith, and tenacity needed to make both your giving and receiving manifestations of God's love for us all.

—Larry Maxwell, President and Chairman of the Board, Century Funds, Inc.

A good fundraiser is invaluable. I know so from experience. With my Doctor Memory learning project for children I've sought out Terry Munday's counsel and support on numerous occasions, always to receive the inspiration and revitalization needed to bring my work to more of those in need. Terry's knowledge and experience would be of great benefit to any fundraising project or organization. Moreover, having pitched in on Terry's fundraising projects with Indiana Wesleyan University, I've seen the benefits of getting involved in the worthy causes of others. Whether speaking at churches, seminars, or golf tournaments for IWU, the joy of being part of something greater than yourself is the ultimate reward. And now, with his *It's Not About the Money*, we can all be part of that something.

—Jerry Lucas, Former New York Knicks National Champion, NCAA Champion at Ohio State University, and U.S Olympic Basketball Team Gold Medalist

ACKNOWLEDGMENTS

When I signed on to work at Indiana Wesleyan University, I had little notion of what was to come or of the kind of people I would meet. But the expectations I had have been surpassed by the wonderful people I have met and worked with over the past two decades. Their spirit and support have inspired me to press on when times were difficult and when I felt ineffective at the university.

I want to thank the university staff, especially those with whom I worked most closely, for their diligent work on our projects over the last 20 years. It is their dedication that has made Indiana Wesleyan so successful. In many ways, they have covered me and made me work better than I was capable of doing and made me more successful than I deserve.

I also want to thank K. Aleisha Fetters for her assistance in writing and organizing the manuscript. Her help with this book was invaluable. Alan Miller, a friend and colleague at IWU, provided editing skills as well. Without the help of these individuals this book would not have been possible.

On the other side of the equation for success, I owe great gratitude to those who have tolerated my requests for donations over the years – and have continued loving me despite my persistence. And now I thank them for allowing me to share their personal stories in this book. I pray that these stories will bring to you a greater understanding of Christian fundraising and, perhaps, even of God's mission for your life.

What's more, when I agreed to take the job at IWU, my wife and children had even less of an understanding of what their futures would hold. They trusted in me, however, and I will always appreciate that. They have stuck by me, enduring my long nights at the office, on the road, or taking time to be with donors at the expense of not being home with them. Through time, the value of their patience has become more apparent to me.

Now that I have seven wonderful grandchildren, and more time to visit with them, I see the moments I did not spend with my children. I fear that they envy the time their children have with me, the time they didn't get from me.

It seems common that those who work to fulfill their obligations to their occupations so often sacrifice the obligations they have to their families. How sad it is that we neglect those who are most dear to us. I have long rationalized that since I was serving God through my work, my absence from home was justified. I know now this is not true.

God forgave me, and God forgives others. Help us, God, always to live according to your vision.

FOREWORD

How do you ask people for money day in and day out — and still believe in generosity? How do you motivate and inspire today's society to give freely of itself for the sake of others?

All fundraisers have asked themselves this at some point during their careers. Terry Munday, former vice president for advancement at Indiana Wesleyan University, is no exception. When he took the position at the small, Christian university, having no fundraising experience, he was overwhelmed with the task before him and his new advancement team: turning a struggling campus into the largest member of the Council for Christian Colleges and Universities.

But they did it. And his *It's Not About the Money* tells how you can do it, too — in your churches, schools, not-for-profits — and wherever else your life may lead you.

Terry's book stands apart from past writings on giving. Until now, such books were limited to the perspective of donors. But Terry has experienced giving from the other side — the side that's making the requests, soliciting donors, and most importantly, seeking God's plan through fundraising. Terry gives every fundraiser — from the Salvation Army bell ringer to the C.E.O. of The Red Cross — the tools to match passion and find success.

In *It's Not About the Money*, Terry guides his readers through his experiences to reveal the true nature of this misunderstood profession — the vision, perseverance, friendships, and generosity. He tells of his personal trials and successes, and the lessons that he took away from both to become a better fundraiser. They will help you grow, too.

It's Not About the Money will change the way you approach charity. Each page will bring you that much closer to fulfilling the mission God has for you and your organization.

—John C. Maxwell
Founder of INJOY Group
Best-selling author of *The 21 Irrefutable Laws of Leadership* and *Leadership Gold*

INTRODUCTION

We plan our lives. But God planned them long ago. If we know what's best for us, we let Him take the lead. That's if we listen — but most of the time that takes some nudging. At least that's true for me.

After spending more than 18 years in the public school circuit serving as a teacher, coach, principal, assistant superintendent, and finally as a superintendent, I was comfortable with my life. I was one of the youngest people to have been named as superintendent of a public school system in Indiana and now I was superintendent of Blackford County Schools, a county school corporation of 2,900 students and 350 faculty and staff members nestled in East Central Indiana. In addition, I was also serving as president of the East Central Indiana Study Council with Ball State University. I was quickly becoming successful at fulfilling my dreams. Despite long hours, I enjoyed the personal touches my career offered me. I had seen children enter the school system and leave as adults. I knew their families. They knew mine.

My wife, Linda, and our four children, Lynn, Shelli, Doug, and Mike, were well provided for by my wages, which allowed Linda to be a stay-at-home wife and mother. We were something of an Ozzie and

Harriet-styled family. And we were happy. For every reason I felt I was in the exact spot God had chosen for my life.

I felt secure — at least until I received a call in June of 1987 from Dr. James Barnes, the President of Indiana Wesleyan University, who asked me to come visit his campus to discuss a job opening at the university. I wasn't familiar with Barnes, but I was with his school. I had graduated there 18 years earlier after transferring from The Ohio State University.

The 1,000-student Wesleyan institution in Marion, Indiana, had a $6 million annual budget with a $500,000 annual deficit. Dr. Barnes knew the university could not survive if that trend continued. He needed someone who could reach out to the larger community to raise funds for the feeble institution.

He wanted me to consider joining this tottering university as the vice president for advancement. My assignment would be to assist in turning around the school's budget, replacing the red ink with gifts that would help the small school not only survive but thrive.

In return for my services he was prepared to offer an annual salary of $30,000, half of what I currently was making as superintendent with the Blackford County School Corporation.

When I left Indiana Wesleyan after my visit, I told Dr. Barnes that I would pray before I made my decision. That was the Christian thing to do. But, in all honesty, I already knew what my answer would be. The salary offer made me yearn for the teacher negotiations, parent meetings, and bus driver disputes that I once hated about my current job. Fundraising: That was near the top of my list of worst jobs I could imagine. My thoughts went back to a hot summer night in 1956. I was eight years old, sitting in a church camp meeting in the middle of a cornfield in Northern Ohio, where I was raised. Even though our family had faithfully attended these meetings for as long as I could remember, and we knew what was about to happen, the plea for money during the service always scared me.

A minister would take to the podium and ask for $1,000. Anyone who was willing to donate the sum would be instructed to stand. The minister then moved through smaller increments, eventually stopping the session by asking everyone who had not yet donated to stand and give $1. *Was that what fundraising really was?* I asked myself. *Is that what Dr. Barnes expected me to do for half of my current salary?*

Of course, I knew that God provides for those who seek His will. I learned that as a child, after returning home from those annual camp meetings. I would watch in fear as my dad emptied out his wallet, and I wondered where my four younger siblings and I were going to get money to buy milk for our cereal during the coming week.

Inevitably Dad, who owned a roofing company, would get an unexpected call the next week offering him a nice roofing job. Dad never failed to give God the credit for those phone calls.

A week later I did the Christian thing: I called Dr. Barnes and told him I hadn't been able to pray through the decision. I hung up the phone and continued on with my life. The next four months were chaotic, yet incredibly fruitful. Negotiations at Blackford County Schools had finally replaced a past teacher strike with a three-year teacher contract that demonstrated the school's new trust. A three-year contract was very rare in the Blackford County School Corporation.

Then the phone rang in my office. "You have a phone call from Dr. Barnes on line one," echoed the voice of my secretary. *Not again*, I thought. Yes, again. Dr. Barnes told me he was being persistent as president of Indiana Wesleyan University, and that the position he offered me four months earlier was still available. The reason seemed clear enough to me.

He asked if I would be willing to return to campus once more and spend an entire day speaking with faculty members, administrators, and anyone I thought could help me reach a final decision on the position. "If you decide after the visit that the position is not the right one for you, I will never bother you again," Dr. Barnes said.

I agreed to the visit.

During my visit professors told me of great opportunities to serve students while faculty and administrators spoke about how blessed they were to work with young people. Now keep in mind, these were people who weren't sure where the next paycheck was coming from! Or if one was coming at all.

I began to realize that the position was greater than me. I knew that I would need the guidance of a higher power if I were to wrestle with all of my doubts about what the future held for me (not to mention wrestling with my ego).

For nearly a month I immersed myself in prayer. I spent sleepless nights tossing and turning in bed. I would wake up, my nightshirt saturated with perspiration, thinking about my two possible realities: the big house, new car, nice clothes… or my family eating lots of spaghetti and living in substandard housing.

God's clarity finally came in the soft voice of my wife: "Maybe we ought to think about what God wants of our lives rather than what we want," Linda said. She said she could get a job to help out with my reduction in income, knowing it would take her away from the home and children she had always held as her life's calling. *Thanks for the dagger*, I thought. Her words went right through my heart. I knew God was directing me to take the job. And I knew I needed to follow His instruction.

After much discussion, the Blackford County School Board accepted my resignation at the end of 1987. The peace I felt was staggering. I began my work at Indiana Wesleyan University in January, 1988.

For the past 18 years as vice president for advancement at IWU, I have seen the once struggling university grow into a booming campus with a $50 million endowment — and no debt.

I have worked as a consultant with many institutions around Indiana and throughout the country conducting capital campaigns, working with direct-mail issues, and addressing other funding concerns. I have counseled churches, Christian schools, community organizations, and other Christian universities that are in financial need.

My rewards have been more than monetary. I have had the opportunity to meet thousands of people who have shaped my understanding of money, giving, and God's spirit. This book is the fruit of those realizations and relationships.

Whether you are a fundraiser for your church, favorite charity, or your children's school, I hope to provide insights into how to approach fundraising in a way that honors God and His people. I have long asked myself how to shamelessly ask people for money. *What makes people see that causes exist that call for our support? What makes them passionate for those causes? How can we be the catalyst for those realizations?*

I believe I finally have my answers.

But this book also is for every person who has struggled over how much to place in the offering plate at church on Sunday morning, for every person who wants to give and feels they can't, and for every person who dreads a phone call from someone looking for funds. *How much should I give? To whom should I give? And, really, why should I give?* The answers are not mine; they come from every person who has written one of my institutions a check with a smile in his or her heart, usually for a reason I can't comprehend.

Only with God's help can I understand both the magnitude and the heart of these people's generosity. And by coming to these realizations only with the wisdom and guidance of my Lord, I have learned that, like most things in life, giving and getting money do not exist in a vacuum. These seemingly worldly acts serve as conduits by which we can ascertain much of God's spirit and desire for our lives and relationships with one another — and with God.

I pray that the lessons I have learned in these past two decades, as well as the stories of those who have taught those lessons, will inspire you as they have me. I encourage you to read the pages that follow with earnestness and trust in God because without God's perseverance in my life, I never would have said yes to the job that has taught me so much and enriched my life. Now I pray it will enrich yours as well.

—Terry Munday

PART 1

DESTIGMATIZING *THE* DIRTY WORD

FUNDRAISING IS THE
GENTLE ART OF TEACHING
THE JOY OF GIVING.

—HANK ROSSO

RELEARNING
THE VALUE *OF*
MONEY

IN THIS CHAPTER
- God's opinion vs. the world's opinion on money
- What does God command us to do with our finances?
- How does God reward generosity?

M any of us have a skewed notion of what fundraising really is. Even more of us simply don't understand what giving is all about. Quite possibly, the reason that we tend to misunderstand charity is because we misunderstand money. But, it's important to make the distinction that money itself is not the issue. Green slips of paper are not intrinsically bad—trust me. The real issue is how we get this money and what we do with it. Our attitude toward money is the problem; the regard we have for it causes an upheaval in both our physical and spiritual

Complete possession is proved only by giving. All you are unable to give possesses you.

—ANDRE GIDE

lives. Money doesn't determine our worth. It doesn't guarantee happiness. In fact, when we hold this regard for money, it can often take the opposite effect in our lives. We are so deeply enmeshed in this world that we don't understand that money is just slips of green paper. As Hebrews explains, the world that we belong to as Christians has a different value system than the material world.

The most important trait for a successful fundraiser to have is an accurate perception of what money and charity mean. That's the truth that we must communicate to our donors. Let's begin there.

WE HAVE SO MUCH TO LEARN

During His time on earth, Jesus said a lot about money. In fact, Jesus talked more about topics such as money than he did about love, humility, kindness... and the list goes on. Fifteen percent of Jesus' recorded words and 13 of His 29 parables are about money and what His followers should do with it. According to Howard Dayton, there are about 500 verses on prayer, 500 verses on faith, and more than 2,300 verses on money and/or possessions (Dayton, 1997).[1] Obviously, it's important to Jesus how we handle our money and possessions.

God knows money can create the illusion that it's all anyone needs when, really, all we need is Him. Scripture says we should understand that money is not ours, but His. We are merely his stewards, or, as I like to think of it, his money managers. Matthew 6:19-20 explains how we, as Christians, should handle His money:

Do not store up for yourselves treasures on earth, where moth and rust destroy, and where thieves break in and steal. But store up for yourselves treasures in heaven, where moth and rust do not destroy, and where thieves do not break in and steal.

Yet, as a whole, we are living much differently than what Matthew describes as our mission — and it's not working for us. Statistics show the over-saturation of materialism in the United States today. By the age of 20, the average American has been exposed to about 1 million advertisements. More people visit the Mall of America than Disney World, the Grand Ole Opry, and the Grand Canyon combined. We like to spend. I heard Doris Donnelly, author and associate professor of theology at John Carroll University in Cleveland, say that as God's disciples we must divest and resist the urge to consume. We must ask ourselves what we truly believe: Does the Gospel or money talk? Does Jesus or money save?

> Remember the Lord your God, for it is he who gives you the ability to produce wealth.
>
> —Deuteronomy 8:18

It has been reported that according to the United States Federal Reserve, nearly 75 percent of U.S. households have credit cards, spurring a credit card debt that now exceeds $10,000 a card. This has sprung from $54 billion in 1980 to $972 billion in 2009. Americans pay interest on $690 billion worth of credit card loans each year. It's estimated that credit card providers would collect more than $19 billion in penalty fees during 2007. Money, which we should use to pay off our mortgages, invest in insurance, and pay healthcare bills, is being lost forever. And it's our doing. We sacrifice the greatest needs in our personal lives for the fad of the day, for materials that can never bring us joy. Forget moths and rust, we are destroying our most precious possessions on our own.

> Many people despise wealth, but few know how to give it away.
>
> —Francois de La Rochefoucauld

We are takers. And God is a giver. He gives rain, food, crops, a Sabbath on which to rest, and so much more. He is our living example of a good and meaningful life. Why can't we as Christians follow His lead when it comes to money?

Because, while in the beginning we were born stewards, we chose to step outside of what was given to us and take what was not intended to be ours. We have claimed false ownership to that which solely belongs to God. This was the sin of Adam and Eve and, thus, of all of us.

As Alan Gotthardt writes in *The Eternity Portfolio*, investing in our families and investing in others are the two pillars of Christian steward-ship (Gotthardt, 2003). As Christians, we understand investing in our families, yet often limit it to our finances. I Timothy 5:8 states that pro-viding for our families requires putting money aside to provide for future needs. We strive to put a strong roof over our children's heads, put their college tuition savings in the bank, etc. Those obligations are not nego-tiable to us. But we fail to implement other means of investing in our families. We fail to invest time. **The average American shops six hours a week and only spends 40 minutes with his or her children.** Obviously, we also need to rework our understanding of the importance of investing in our families. We must take the time to be with our families and to show our love for them. We must share Christian lessons and prin-ciples with our children. This is the foundation of making our world the world that He designed.[2]

If we fail to make time for our families, it's no wonder that we don't make time to invest in others. Still, we make time for our other priorities. I was recently told about a survey that was conducted by the Archdiocese of Detroit that we make time to watch an average of 12 hours of TV a week in America. We spend four hours watching movies and reading for pleasure, spend three hours on hobbies and another two hours on exercise. These are all predominantly solitary activities. While spending time alone with God is an incredibly rewarding activity, we also need to balance our lives by spend-ing time in community and fellowship. We weren't made to be alone. We were made to live in community with one another and to show God's love to all. We must reach out, being aware of the needs in our neighborhoods and our world. God promises blessings to those who freely give of them-selves. It will not only enrich the lives of others, but yours as well.

In I Corinthians 12: 4-7, Paul says that we all are endowed with unique and meaningful gifts. My wife has the gift of cooking. She uses her talent to show members of our church and community that she cares about them. A warm dish for children whose mother has just entered the hospital or a family who has just lost a loved one does help to warm the soul. It shows others that she cares about them as God cares about all of His children. By demonstrating that love to others, we make earth a bit more like Heaven.

God understands that focusing our efforts and passions on Him rather than on money is more than a demonstration of faith. In Matthew 6, verses 21 and 24, Jesus explains that investing in God's Kingdom ultimately determines the direction of our hearts and our faith in God:

"For where your treasure is, there your heart will be also." He continues, "No one can serve two masters... You cannot serve both God and Money."

If we want to live both by His example and with a heart for Him, we must give. When we give, we learn to trust God with our earthly belongings and surrender them to Him. We learn to realize that we have many blessings that are not merely the fruits of our labor. Salaries come with our work, but it is God who gives us the ability and drive to work. Work comes with life, but God grants us life. Without Him, our lives would not be possible. Selfless giving is how we can best demonstrate and better understand that relationship.

It is every man's obligation to put back into the world at least the equivalent of what he takes out of it.

—ALBERT EINSTEIN

God owns all of our money. He can take it away or give it anytime He wants. If we truly believe God owns it all, every spending decision is a spiritual decision.

WHAT SHOULD WE DO?

Further His mission and glorify Him.

When hoarded for our own enjoyment and benefit, money loses its charm. But when we help others, and use it to spread His love throughout the world, money is so much more than dollars and cents.

> Giving opens the way for receiving.
> —FLORENCE SCOVEL SHINN

Scripture commands us to give 10 percent of our income to His mission. Some people feel that the 10 percent rule is an Old Testament principle and does not apply to modern Christians. We often feel that we should give only what we want — our hearts have to be in it, after all. We often cite the New Testament's teaching of giving based on need and ability, and give this as our excuse for giving only what we choose. And we have chosen much less than what we can give. According to an article by Rob Moll in *Christianity Today*, 10 percent of evangelical Protestants give nothing at all to any form of charity, while 36 percent give away less than 2 percent of their income. Only 27 percent tithe.[3] This level represents an all-time low in religious giving. And it's not because we can't afford to give. As Joel Belz notes, we Americans are by no means the generous, giving people we like to imagine. We could double our giving by managing our finances responsibly as God commands, and still live lifestyles that are relatively similar to the ones to which we've grown accustomed. Many of us could double our giving and still fall short of the tithe that God instructed His people to consider the starting point. We ask why our schools and churches aren't doing more to serve. We are the answer.

But still, we don't trust God with our money. "Test me now," God said through Malachi. "See if I won't open the windows of Heaven, and pour you out a blessing so big you won't be able to

> If every American donated five hours a week, it would equal the labor of 20 million full-time volunteers.
> —CLAUDE ROSENBERG

receive it." (Malachi 3:10 *The Message*) Most of us are too scared to actually take the test.[4] We think that if we put a $20 bill in the offering plate on Sunday, we will lose $20. But we will really gain so much more. God has promised to take care of us if we trust in Him, and the simple act of giving to God is an amazing step of faith that God loves to reward.

THE REWARDS OF GIVING

If all American Christians gave according to their ability and to God's command in scripture, annual giving by Christians would be about at $85.5 billion. $10 billion would provide care for 20 million children for a year. $330 million would back 150,000 missionaries in countries closed to religious workers. $2.2 billion would triple the funding of Bible translation, printing, and distribution. $600 million would start eight Christian colleges in Eastern Europe and Southeast Asia. We would change the world with $85.5 billion. We would change the world if we just followed God's commandment to give.

When we think of others first as God has commanded, there's no other option than to give. If we learn to love others as God loves us, we will be more generous than we ever thought possible.

As fundraisers, it is our responsibility to mentor, disciple, and facilitate donors in developing generous hearts for God. It's impossible to be a fundraiser without also being a giving person. Friends and associates have often teased me for having a soft spot for students in need or for organizations in financial rough spots. I'm glad to have that soft spot; I owe it to God. I want to be a living example of generous and selfless giving. Throughout our history, the true Christian response to human need has been one of the best advertisements for our faith. Christ will judge and reward us for our giving to others out of love. We are not exempt from God's rule of giving — thank goodness. Giving is well worth it.

KEY TAKEAWAYS:

- All money ultimately belongs to God. When we remember that, we seek to glorify God with our finances, strengthening our faith along the way.
- Investing in our families and others, both financially and spiritually, are pillars of Christianity. They are pillars we often forget. We get caught up in our day-to-day lives, but it's time to get back, and help others get back, to living lives based in Christ's love for others.
- Fundraisers must lead lives that serve as examples of Godly charity and giving. If it is done right, giving is contagious.

CHAPTER 2

FUNDRAISING (MISUNDERSTOOD)

IN THIS CHAPTER
- To surmount your obstacles as a fundraiser, first identify them
- Stigmas plague us
- How to bring about change in the hearts of others

I n *The Eternity Portfolio*, Gotthardt writes, "…many people resent that pastors and non-profit organizations always seem to be asking for money. The modest giving that does occur is more often from a sense of habit or guilt than from purpose or compassion…"[1] Unfortunately, this is very true. And there are plenty of reasons for it.

WHAT ARE THE ROOTS OF OUR OBSTACLES?

A personal survey of fundraisers for the Council for Christian Colleges and Universities, which represents 110 institutions of Christian higher education in the United States, found that one of the main reasons that prospective donors object to giving is that the charitable organization is asking for too much money. Since the requesting organizations have most often done their homework in evaluating what amount of money an individual can and cannot give, how can we explain this objection?

No one has ever become poor by giving.

—ANNE FRANK

We often forget that donors have real concerns for their families' livelihoods. Potential donors are often reluctant to give money that would otherwise be given to their children and grandchildren. The value of an inheritance is high on the priority list to those born in the earlier part of the 20th century. During their adolescence, it was this money that helped to sustain them after their parents' passing. They feel that passing down a similar inheritance is both their obligation and their legacy.

Potential donors' children are also concerned about the estate of their parents and often will become a part of the decision-making process for older donors. Children do not want to see their parents give away the money for which they worked throughout their younger years. Children want to see their parents enjoy their retirement, and rightly so.

He who is kind to the poor lends to the Lord, and He will reward him for what he has done.

—PROVERBS 19:17

Children, however, do not only have concerns for their parents, but also for themselves. **According to Giving USA, by the year 2050, an estimated $41 trillion will transfer from one generation to the next in the form of inheritances.**[2] The younger generation has a large stake in that sum. If they have foreseen a large inheritance coming from their parents or grandparents, they naturally do not want to see it given away. They don't want to lose the money on which they've been banking — sometimes for decades. On occasion, I have even had donors' children step into negotiations to prohibit part of their inheritance from being donated to IWU. Once I was called to a man's office because he wanted to make a $1 million gift. I had been working with the gentleman for a year or so on this gift. But upon arriving at his office, I was confronted by his grandson and an attorney who said they would not permit the donor to make the gift. I immediately sensed that I was in the midst of a family dispute, and I graciously excused myself from the decision.

Many children do not know how to give as they should because their parents are failing to set the example or teach them the value of giving to others. I become ecstatic when I find that my young grandchildren have accepted a charge to give to our church's building fund. My grandchildren understand that to build the church, everyone needs to do his or her part. Parents are doing something right when children are thinking of others. Starting this understanding and passion at an early age will only prove to enrich their lives, as well as the lives of others, as they mature.

After concerns for their own wellbeing, potential donors are restricted from giving by their own misconceptions. These are very real concerns for donors. Although they may seem irrational or even selfish, we must learn to acknowledge them if we are to surmount them. It is our job to assist people in understanding God's purpose.

BAD IMPRESSIONS

A stigma exists from elementary school days when we (as our children and grandchildren today) were required to sell candy, magazines, candles, and other items to fund everything from a school field trip to blankets for the local homeless shelter. Personally, my definition of fundraising was formed during my childhood revival days when a preacher stood on a platform and demanded — in front of the congregation — that everyone make a donation.

"Stand up if you are willing to give $1,000," he would say.

There was no secret or humility about the giving. Nor was there any "don't let your left hand know what your right hand is doing." Just as that memory is fresh in my mind, the memories of childhood fundraising are fresh in the minds of our donors. These memories are often more negative than positive.

These experiences sour us on the whole process of fundraising — at least as we understand the process. We understand fundraising as an impersonal act, a sort of business transaction that somehow exploits everyone involved: from the kids walking door to door in the snow, to the neighbors who buy overpriced candy and fruit baskets they don't want. Then, we see only a small fraction of the earnings go to the cause for which it was intended. No wonder we have grown up with a distrust of fundraising. When prompted to give, we ask ourselves, *Will my money be used as directed or used to line someone's pockets? Will it be wasted? Can I trust giving this organization the money for which I have worked?* The doubts and questions flood our minds and hearts.

Harris Interactive DonorPulse cites "one-third of U.S. adults as having less than positive feelings towards America's charitable organizations." Only 10 percent of the respondents believe that charitable organizations are honest and ethical in their use of donations.[3]

Unfortunately, there are a few bad apples in every bushel, and their mismanagement of funds has given fundraising a bad rap. In California, the attorney general's office reports that during the last decade, fundraisers for nonprofits kept more than 94 cents of every dollar that was donated. In a 2008 investigatory piece in the *Los Angeles Times*, Doug Smith and Charles Piller found similar findings:

- More than 100 charities raised $1 million or more from commercial appeals, but more than 75 cents of each dollar raised was spent on appeals.
- In 430 U.S. fundraising campaigns, charities received nothing: all $44 million donated went to the fundraisers. In 337 of those cases, charities actually lost money.

- Missing-children charities received less than 15 percent of the more than $28 million raised on their behalf.[4]

It's crucial as a fundraiser to value money enough to not spend it on wasteful tactics. Our organization, Indiana Wesleyan University, in its direct-mail campaign, has tried to hold expenses to 20 cents for every dollar raised. That means the causes of our direct-mail solicitations receive at least 80 percent of the money raised.

We must also be mindful of the perceptions that we communicate to donors. On one occasion I was called to the local Chevrolet-Cadillac dealership in the university's hometown of Marion. I had contacted the dealership and asked the manager, Joe Clement, if the business would furnish a car or van for me as I represented the university in the community and across the United States. Joe said that he had talked with the owner, Jim DeVoe, and they had decided to furnish me with a vehicle. As we headed across the showroom floor, Joe pointed to a new white Cadillac with all the trimmings. Joe said, since you are traveling around the community we want to put you in a nice car. My immediate response was to take it — obviously. But after a minute or so I looked at Joe and told him that I appreciated this wonderful gesture but felt that my potential donors would get the wrong impression if I were to drive up to their homes with this beautiful car. I left that day, hoping that Joe understood my position and my gratitude. The clientele that I was serving were largely alumni and individuals in the helping professions (teachers, preachers, social workers, etc.) who could not afford such high-end cars. I had to be sensitive to their concerns and decline the Cadillac.

A week later, I called Joe to thank him for his generous offer of the car and hoped that he understood the reason for my hesitance. Joe immediately suggested that I come out to see him. I drove over and again met with Joe. When he appeared, we walked out to the car lot and he asked, "Terry, could you drive that new Chevrolet Venture van?" I could do that. Absolutely. For the next 15 years, the dealership furnished me with a new van to drive as part of my job responsibilities.

It is important to practice good Christian stewardship when raising funds for a Christian cause. We must be good stewards for the sake of our causes, our donors, and our recipients. Still, many organizations exist that do not value donors' money as they should, and these groups have tarnished the reputations of not-for-profits nationwide. Paul C. Light, professor of public service at New York University, says, "Charities may be losing their most prized possession: their reputation for caring."[5] Their stories have been shown on TVs across America as the Federal Government investigates their wasteful spending. My survey of the alumni of the Council of Christian Colleges and Universities found that only half have positive feelings towards fundraising. This is the percentage of the population that is the most likely to have a positive view of fundraising and giving because they were taught Christian values. When we look at the segment of the population that was not taught to love others above themselves, or to give generously, the figures only get worse. Americans have lost faith in giving.

BE THE CHANGE

What does all this doubt mean to Christian fundraisers? It means that we are working with people who are caught up in the "keeping-up-with-the-Joneses" syndrome and don't know it. We are working with people who think we are pickpockets in business attire, looking out for our own interests above theirs.

> Everyone thinks of changing the world, but no one things of changing himself.
>
> —Leo Nikolaevich Tolstoy

Fundraising can become a big business in all organizations, including Christian ones, and that is a distortion of its purpose. Its aim is to help further God's mission through our institutions with the involvement and support of ordinary people.

Fortunately, there is hope for us as Christian fundraisers. As those making the requests for money, we have a certain amount of control over the concerns of our donors. We can gain their confidence and trust. We can show them the mission of our organizations and how their generosity can help to achieve our goals. Giving USA suggests that the following fundraising strategies should be considered:

- Build a more compelling case for giving. There are more than one million non-profit organizations vying for donor dollars.
- Improve communications with donors through regular newsletters and emails.
- Gain a broader audience by partnering with other organizations.
- Improve efforts in getting small annual gifts from your constituents.
- Increase attention concerning the needs of your organization.
- Shift priorities from fundraising to solving specific problems within the community.[6]

Most importantly, we never should abandon our donors or misguide the trust they have in us. We are not only serving the interests of our organization. As Christians, we are serving the interests of everyone with whom we come in contact.

We should be prepared to give people something in return for the money they give our organizations. We must invest in them for the long term and show that we care about more than their money. Many television evangelists have taken advantage of people by presenting themselves as agents of God who can solve a problem if they will send a check. Water (supposedly) from the Jordan River, prayer handkerchiefs, and other trinkets are all they receive. There are no calls, no meetings, no friendships, and no knowledge of what becomes of their donations.

> Life is an echo—what you send out comes back.
>
> —UNKNOWN

Our responsibility as fundraisers does not stop at collecting checks and seeing to their proper management. Since we are Christian fundraisers, it is also our responsibility to teach them how to give, and help them to deepen their faith through giving. To relieve the concerns of donors, you must show them yourself and your heart for God's mission. **When teaching others how to give, you must show them their own soul and bend it in God's direction.** Obviously, the latter is the more difficult task set before fundraisers. But, it is possible with sincerity and love.

God alone can give us the ability to love others as He does, and it is the fundraiser's responsibility to pray and seek Him in earnest.

We cannot expect all givers to be the cheerful stewards that God (and every fundraiser) loves. Sometimes they only can be the obedient stewards that God loves. We should love them, as well. More often than not, donors are simply human, unwilling to give without proper incentive. My personal survey of the Council for Christian Colleges and Universities, for example, reveals that often individuals and institutions give to their schools for personal motives. These incentives fluctuate from rewards on earth to those in Heaven.

So if we allow our donors to give based on rewards and incentives, is that selfish of us, or of them? Not necessarily. God understands man's heart and how we assess our good deeds. God programmed us with a need for positive reinforcement. All of our good deeds on earth will be rewarded in Heaven. And God is happy to reward.

As Randy Alcorn writes in *Money, Possessions, and Eternity*, these rewards are often a springboard to generosity. This cycle of giving and fruition causes the donor to begin giving as Christ has commanded, with love for others and a desire to see his or her money further God's mission.[7]

> You make a living by what you get. You make a life by what you give.
>
> —WINSTON CHURCHILL

Dr. Thomas Kinnan, pastor of Breakpoint Community Church in Kansas, poses another model for Christians' levels of generosity and how they develop over time. He contends that giving increases with one's spiritual maturity. **Mature Christians reflect a greater understanding of the love and generosity of God.** Through one's walk, the Holy Spirit becomes a further agent of change in the hearts of Christians. Many Christians begin giving for self-preservation — to reduce their taxes, for example. Perhaps more often, donors give out of a sense of moral obligation, feeling he or she must do so in order to win "brownie points" with God and others. Many more give based on their ease — and even implied force — of doing so: for example, to Salvation Army bell ringers and to Girl Scouts selling cookies. We feel we have to give, and once we do we feel all warm and fuzzy inside. In the end, we like it. Eventually we move to a philanthropic standpoint. As Luke 12:48 says, "From everyone who has been given, much will be demanded and with one who has been entrusted with much, much more will be asked." Once we begin to submit to the reality of our world's needs, we are motivated by compassion, and then love. This is true Christ-like giving: giving with no thought of personal adulation or personal sacrifice. We value community, family, and life above our own material desires.[8]

This concept indicates to me why so many people are not charitable and do not want a fundraiser or someone representing a cause to approach them: they have not matured in their spiritual lives to the point of being true stewards. In fact, many have become so bogged down in their personal finances that they cannot move anywhere but down the rungs of giving.

> No person was ever honored for what he received. Honor has been the reward for what he gave.
>
> —CALVIN COOLIDGE

We must demonstrate that the giver needs the experience of giving as badly as the organization needs the joy of receiving the gift. For example, Dr. Ron Jones had been somewhat sporadic in his giving until he experienced the joy of giving to the spring and summer missions programs at our university. As he received the reports of the lives that were being changed — both those being served and the students themselves — he decided to invest his entire estate in the program. Ron and his wife, Marge, have not only become faithful givers, they have also become earnest in their prayer lives for the students who are benefiting from their giving. In our associations with other donors, such as one IWU alumnus and one South Carolina pastor, we have had to tell them to refrain from giving in order to protect their own interests. Some donors so love to see the impact of their gifts that they think almost too selflessly.

Van Gurley knows that giving is a process. Once you surrender the gift to God, He will bless it. In this instance, Van owned a property that had been used as a car lot in Brazil, Indiana. He had been trying to sell the lot for more than a year when he decided to donate it to IWU. Shortly after we visited the location and saw its strategic location next to a Ford dealership and directly across the street from a Chrysler dealership, I decided to approach the Ford dealer, Dan Bowen, to determine his interest. I told him that I had a property that he needed, and since he was located adjacent to the property, I wanted to give him the first chance to purchase it. If he was not interested, I was going across the street to give the Chrysler dealer the same opportunity.

Dan's immediate reply was, "You know I have been thinking about that property. How much do you want for it?" Since I had not fully discussed a price with Van, I suggested a price range of between $240,000 and $290,000.

"I will call you in the morning," Dan said.

The next morning I received a telephone call confirming that Dan would pay a price that was higher than the Realtor had listed it for previously. Because the property had moved so quickly, I suggested that I step aside and allow Van to accept the money. But Van insisted that this was a "God thing. It was God's money." How true he was.

The money has served countless university students in need of financial assistance. Recently, after Van had visited his daughter, a freshman on campus, he called me on his way home and said, "Terry, I just want to tell you I am thinking of you and want to thank you for this beautiful campus. I see your fingerprints everywhere. It has been two weeks since we brought our daughter to the campus, and I already notice a difference in her spiritual walk." How far we had come since the days I first called on Van, not knowing how wonderful our relationship would become over the next decade.

Selfless giving cannot be accomplished in our own strength. It is only possible through the internal work of the Holy Spirit. This sense of mission is ultimately our goal to convey to those with whom we work. We must show our donors that their money is larger than them or us, or anything that we can imagine.

KEY TAKEAWAYS:

- Donors have real concerns for their families' livelihoods. We must understand and appreciate them if we are going to surmount them.
- Unfortunately, a few fundraisers have perpetuated a stigma of fundraisers being untrustworthy among Americans. We need to be sensitive to this reputation to show potential donors that we are honest and sincere in our campaigns.
- Our responsibility to donors does not stop at collecting checks. It is also our responsibility to teach them how to give and help them to deepen their faith through giving. We should help donors meet their personal needs and extend Christ's love to them.
- Dr. Thomas Kinnan, pastor of Breakpoint Community Church in Kansas, believes that giving increases with one's spiritual maturity and vice versa. Thus, as we guide potential donors in Christian giving, we also guide their spirituality and faith.

PART 2

INTESTINAL
FORTITUDE

CONFIDENCE IS PREPARATION.
EVERYTHING ELSE IS
BEYOND YOUR CONTROL.

—Richard Kline

LOSE
ALL PRIDE

IN THIS CHAPTER
- Taking advantage of opportunities
- Going to extremes to secure funds
- Being bold with your trust in God

M oney is a kind of all-powerful, unmentionable in our society, something polite people don't talk about, but always think about. Society encourages us to accumulate as much money and possessions as possible while not discussing our small fortunes with anyone — let alone strangers. Being the stranger who is making outright requests for gifts can be intimidating.

As Christians, we hear the "lose all pride" sermon all of the time. From childhood picture Bibles to

Humble yourselves, therefore, under the mighty hand of God so that at the proper time he may exalt you, casting all your anxieties on him, because he cares for you.

—1 PETER 5:5–7

family mission trips, our experiences instruct us to depress our often over-inflated egos and to deny our vanity. Matthew 23:12 says, "For whoever exalts himself will be humbled, and whoever humbles himself will be exalted." Even at the most basic level, this humility is completely against our prideful nature. But as Christian fundraisers, this humility is in our job description.

SEIZING OPPORTUNITIES

Make the most of every opportunity. Let your conversation be always full of grace, seasoned with salt, so that you may know how to answer everyone.

—Colossians 4:5–6

To be successful fundraisers, we must push past our own self-importance. Pride keeps us in line with decorum, while humility does not. Take Indiana Wesleyan University's annual Grandparents Day, for example. Each fall, the university welcomes nearly 650 grandparents of our students to the campus for a day in their honor. In September 2002, like every other year, we planned a tour of our beautiful campus so the grandparents could enjoy the bright colors of Indiana autumn. The grandparents then would sit in our classrooms to witness our Christian teaching philosophy and style. They would meet faculty members and administrators whose mission was to guide their grandchildren through their higher education. These activities were just one way to create a family-oriented atmosphere in which our visitors could realize the importance of a Christian environment for their grandchildren. Nowhere in our jam-packed schedule for the weekend did we write down a time to ask our guests for money.

Of course, since the grandparents were members of our extended campus community, we knew that the grandparents cared a great deal about the institution and its welfare. But promoting the university from a financial standpoint just wasn't on our agenda for Grandparents Day. Frankly, we decided that asking grandparents for donations was an ill-mannered move. We wanted to welcome them, not appear as vultures ready for the strike.

A few months before one Grandparents Day, we received a letter from Lilly Endowment, Inc., an Indianapolis-based philanthropic organization. The letter informed us of a challenge for Indiana college alumni and relatives of current students. For every dollar those donors gave, the Endowment would provide a matching dollar. I did the math quickly: This meant that every dollar we received from grandparents on this day would automatically double. It was undeniably an enormous opportunity for IWU to raise money for its students.

After a few weeks of consideration, I knew what I had to do. I had to put God's calling — and the opportunity He had provided me — above my pride. Honestly, I didn't want to stand in front of our hundreds of guests and ask them to give the university money. But, I knew this was an opportunity that only came once a year, and I needed to seize the moment. Now I had to take it regardless of whether it was ill mannered, improper, or downright rude. I was about to shift the decorum for this annual event. I would ask the grandparents to donate money for our scholarship fund.

Preparing for the appeal, I thought through the logistics. Suddenly, the gravity of the already stellar opportunity struck me. The Indiana State Tax Credit for Higher Education would make the grandparents' donations go even further. Since about 60 percent of the IWU student body comes from Indiana, it was logical to assume that the vast majority of the visiting grandparents also would be from the Hoosier state. These family members would, therefore, qualify for Indiana tax credit with their donations. If they gave $400, the state would return $200 of that donation as a tax credit. By taking the $400 as an itemized deduction on Federal income tax returns, the actual cost of the $400 gift fell below $100. On top of that, the Lilly Endowment would then double the gift to $800.

The bottom line: An out-of-pocket expense of less than $100 would generate an $800 gift for Indiana Wesleyan — an amazing return on stewardship.

So when I stood before the grandparents, I resolved to make Christian stewardship the focus of my request. I sought a humorous way to break the ice — while preparing them for the fact that I ultimately was going to ask for money.

"I've been having dreams," I said. "In fact, last night I dreamed that I went to heaven. St. Peter met me at the pearly gate and said, 'I have three questions for you before you are admitted. First, do you have the IWU license plate on your car? (We were always seeking ways to get our alumni and friends to outwardly show their loyalty to the school with vanity license plates offered by the State of Indiana.) Second, have you taken advantage of the Indiana Tax Credit for Higher Education? And, third, have you made a contribution that will count toward the Lilly Endowment Challenge?'"

The crowd erupted in laughter, and I knew the grandparents then felt comfortable with my appeal for money. Now I shifted my focus to tell the grandparents of the great opportunity they had to be good Christian stewards — whether they lived in Indiana or another state. The response was heartwarming as we distributed free IWU golf umbrellas to grandparents who said they would join us in our pursuit of the Lilly Challenge. Ironically, as grandparents left the Performing Arts Center that day it began to rain. When people began to open their new umbrellas because of an act of God, it seemed to confirm that asking them for money was the right thing to do.

Later that day, a couple approached me in the Performing Arts Center. They introduced themselves as Herb and Donna Rickert, grandparents of one of our students. This was their first visit to campus. They explained that they were impressed with IWU's Christian spirit and grateful that their grandchildren were being educated in such an environment. Standing there with tears in his eyes, Herb handed me a check for $10,000. **I immediately heard God speaking through this gentleman, assuring me that I had done the right thing in asking for donations.** The Biblical admonition, "You have not because you ask not," was clear. Good thing I had asked!

The following year, Herb returned for Grandparents Day, with a thankful and grateful heart and provided us with a check for $20,000. He said he wanted to replenish the funds that he had given the previous year because he knew that money had been spent. To date, Herb and Donna, have donated more than $135,000 to the university. He has helped students to become pastors, business owners, and doctors. He has helped to give worthy students their futures.

DO WHATEVER IT TAKES

After I joined the Indiana Wesleyan University team, we began an annual fundraising telesale that aired for four hours a night, five consecutive nights on our campus television station. During 20 hours of live television which was carried on cable TV systems in surrounding counties, we auctioned off items — both grand and mundane — to raise money for student scholarships. We accepted almost any auction items that our community offered, and more than 300 community volunteers — many of them on TV for the first time — helped to sell those items. The IWU telesale quickly became a successful and celebrated event by our community. The first telesale raised $15,000. By the 10th year, the telesale was raising $165,000 annually for student scholarships.

During the five nights of the telesale, the two dozen phones on our phone bank occasionally fell silent. That was my cue to pull some antics out of my sleeves. It seemed that the crazier I acted in front of the camera, the more people called with bids. Most of the antics were spontaneous with little time to think. People would see me in downtown Marion or in the local mall and say, "I've never seen that side of you!"

Trust in the Lord with all your heart, and lean not on your own understanding; In all your ways acknowledge Him and He shall direct your paths.

—PROVERBS 3:5–6 (NKJV)

While I really had no way of knowing the tangible effect of my actions on the auction, I could sense them, from our total profits to our ringing phones. When there were lulls in the action, the stage manager, Dr. Scott

Turcott, would faithfully scream backstage, "Get Munday out here! We need some life in this show, it's dying!" That was my cue to grab any prop that went with the auction item and get to work. If it was a ladder, I'd climb the ladder singing, "Climb every mountain, forge every stream, follow every rainbow." If it were a tricycle, I would ride it across the stage. If it were a hair salon visit, I would strut across our stage modeling a wonderfully awful wig. At one point, we even auctioned off a toilet (I said we would auction anything that was donated to us!), and I grabbed a newspaper, opened it up and sat down. For almost any item that we sold, I could find something funny to keep our viewers entertained — and, most importantly, to get the item sold.

OPPORTUNITIES, REVISITED

A few years after our first success with the Lilly Challenge, we received word again that the endowment would match donations made to Indiana colleges and universities. This time the incentive was even greater: for every $1 Indiana Wesleyan raised, Lilly Endowment would give us $1.50 — up to a maximum of $3.5 million. The money only could come from alumni, friends, family members and Indiana Wesleyan employees. At that time, our alumni were giving about $400,000 a year, so raising $3.5 million was considered more than a stretch for our advancement team.

Wracking my brain for an antic like ones I had used on the telesale, I remembered how I had watched our students break the ice on the school pond and take a swim in the winter. Students were fascinated with the event. *What if I could get 10 donors to sponsor me at $10,000 each to take the plunge myself?* Not only would that raise $100,000, but $250,000 since the Lilly Endowment would match it. I already had secured a list of potential donors when my cardiologist informed me that I should not be involved in such a stunt. Although disappointed by the news, just talking about the gimmick helped us reach our $3.5 million goal and receive the full match from the Lilly Endowment.

We modified the original "plunge" idea for our annual chaparral, a trip where we take senior citizens to Colonial American settings (Williamsburg, Washington D.C., Charleston S.C., Gettysburg, etc.). Making fun of my earlier plan to take the ice plunge, we asked the seniors to indicate how much they would give if I sat in a kiddy pool of ice water. In an effort to make it as monumental as possible, I dressed in goggles, fins and a wet suit, flopping my way to the pool. It was a hoot, and the group responded by giving $8,000 to the scholarship fund. People think I will do almost anything to raise funds. Perhaps, but we also raised a lot of fun along the way.

> Money is not given, It has to be raised. Money is not offered, It has to be asked for, Money does not come in, It must be gone after.
>
> —ANONYMOUS

HOLY BOLDNESS

Once you get old you can say anything, or so I've heard. So, when donor Dick Anthony, a 74-year-old owner of Indiana Mills and Manufacturing Inc., a large seat belt and child restraint manufacturer, told me that *I* was bold, I was little less than dumbfounded. The man claimed I was "the best fundraiser" he ever had dealt with because I had what he called "holy boldness." After our conversation, I began to contemplate his words. *Was that true? Was I really so bold? And was that my key asset as a fundraiser?* The answer to all three questions was, yes. But it wasn't *my* asset; it was God's asset shown through me. **For me — and for every fundraiser — boldness should take the form of our trust in God.** We are unwavering because our strength is God's. And then our confidence, strength, and boldness are above our pride, our agendas, and ourselves.

They all belong to God.

As Christians, we all learn this at different times in our lives. My lesson came when I began working with IWU. I had no previous fundraising experience, but I had a desire to help secure funds quickly. I decided to take a door-to-door approach in the business community. Since most of the businesses were located on the Marion bypass, I started a Grant County Scholarship Day by asking each business owner to consider a gift of $200 to $500. I was able to make between 20 and 25 calls a day and, in some cases, schedule meetings for the following day. I will agree that this is not high quality, research-based fundraising, but it helped me to know the community and individuals who could partner with the university.

During those long days of making cold calls, the devil often would come and tell me I was a failure, and that my three academic degrees were being wasted. I was a failure in the eyes of the university, myself, and even my family. Despite the temptations, however, I saw the program start to succeed as businesses began giving, and people gained knowledge of what was happening in the university. The Grant County Scholarship drive became so successful that we decided to do the same thing in an adjoining county. Fundraising can be tough on the ego at times.

When we embrace God's strength, we also embrace His candor. They act as a sensible and powerful pair of attributes. That's why, as a general rule, to be good fundraisers we should request donations in person. We then have the opportunity to show prospective donors some of the life and meaning behind our causes. They are no longer ink on paper. They are real. But in order to guarantee this personal contact, you must take the initiative and develop a strategy. When I first requested money from the Fortune Foundation, a private, Indianapolis-based foundation started by W. Brooks Fortune, the proposal had to be submitted in writing. I decided to compensate for that disadvantage by asking to deliver the proposal to Dr. and Mrs. Fortune in person. I phoned the couple and explained that I wished to meet with them to tell them about our university and to answer any questions they might have about Indiana Wesleyan's mission. They agreed to allow me to deliver the request to them at their home. But little did I expect that a genial, smiling Mrs. Wanda Fortune would meet me at the door and warmly welcome me into her living room where her husband, a gentleman in his 80s, was seated. They appeared genuinely appreciative and interested in having me in their home. We sat talking amid their family portraits and memorabilia. What an unusual, but welcoming, environment to ask the couple for $10,000 for IWU. Boldness does often yield staggering results.

I had chosen to seek funds for our adult nursing program, which we had been working hard to promote at the time. The program catered to adults who, after raising their own families, now wished to serve others through the nursing profession. The need was real, selfless, and close to Wanda's heart. Several decades earlier, she had been trained as a nurse. Brooks Fortune was also interested in health care as a result of his long career as a chemist and group vice president with Eli Lilly and Company.

> Fortune befriends the bold.
>
> —JOHN DRYDEN

A month later, I received a letter stating that the proposal had been approved by the Fortunes and that we would be receiving the $10,000 grant we had requested from their foundation. That money was followed by an increasingly personal relationship with the Fortunes, which allowed me to visit the couple on my frequent trips to Indianapolis. A piece of pie or a few cookies became part of my visits, and we often shared stories and laughter over lunch. Within a few months, the Fortunes were asking about my wife and children by name.

It was at this point in our friendship that I asked them if I could give them a tour of Indiana Wesleyan University's campus. They had never seen the institution that their gift had benefited, and I felt that our relationship was the best bridge to lead them to the Marion campus. I picked them up at their home in Indianapolis and drove them the 60 miles to our rapidly growing campus. We had recently completed a new science building. Because of the Fortunes' special interest in health and medicine, and in an effort to keep their walking to a minimum, I chose to skip several of our buildings so we could focus on the Burns Hall of Science and Nursing. The building houses the chemistry, biology, and physics laboratories as well as the nursing laboratories and classrooms.

After taking the Fortunes on a tour of the building's new state-of-the-art simulation labs, I stepped in front of the door and said, "Brooks and Wanda, to the right of this door would be a great place for a picture and plaque that reads, "The Brooks and Wanda Fortune Simulation Laboratory." Brooks gave me a sly grin, confirming he did, in fact, understand the shameless request I had just made. "What would that cost me?" he asked.

"$50,000," I replied.

Nothing more was mentioned about the request for the rest of the day. But during my next visit to the Fortunes' home, Brooks looked at Wanda and gave her the cue to write me a check for $50,000. A few moments later, the check was in my hand.

My relationship with the Fortunes began with a desire to ask for a seemingly simple financial gift. And it blossomed into a friendship that allowed for daring appeals to benefit a worthy cause. It's important to note that while always being honest with the couple, I made my bold request in the simulation laboratory only after having built a trusting relationship with Brooks and Wanda (a skill we will further discuss in Part 3).

In 2005, I received a telephone call from Wanda. She told me that Brooks had passed away. She requested that the university's president and I participate in the funeral. At the funeral we were seated near the front of the sanctuary with the family. The former chairman of the board of Eli Lilly, former president of Purdue University, the president of Mount Union College, the president of Christian Theological Seminary, and the president of IWU shared words of tribute. Following the service we were invited to join the family for lunch.

About three months later, I received a telephone call from Dr. John Fortune, the son of Brooks. He said that his father had developed a unique friendship with IWU and with me, and that Brooks loved the university's mission. He noted that he was saddened to inform me that the $20,000 annual nursing scholarship that his father had started would not continue with the passing of his father. That was understandable, but he continued, "A year ago, my father set up a Charitable Trust for IWU and within the next year IWU will be receiving a gift of $425,000 to $450,000." Immediately, emotion overtook me as tears fell to my desk. A relationship that started only eight to 10 years earlier had developed into a friendship that exceeded my wildest expectations. God is so good!

Sometimes there is not time to build that foundation. You simply must act. Although terrifying, it is possible to come out of such situations with success. That was the case when the university president, Dr. Jim Barnes, entered my office with a troubled look on his face. Sitting down across the desk from me, he explained his dilemma — actually our dilemma. Fifty-six acres of land across from the university, a parcel that we had kept an eye on for several years, needed to be acquired for campus development. The property was not even for sale, nor did we have the money to buy it. In addition, a developer had recently completed the final home in the housing addition adjacent to the property, and he would be a prime candidate to buy the land in which we had an interest.

While I have no qualms about housing developments, the possibility of these homes posed a particular threat to Indiana Wesleyan, which was just starting to expand its campus and was building a residence hall each year to accommodate the steady growth of students. Where would we go if a development started encroaching on the land we knew the University eventually would need?

For the Lord GOD will help me; therefore shall I not be confounded: therefore have I set my face like a flint; and I know that I shall not be ashamed.

—Isaiah 50:7 (KJV)

At the president's urging, I scheduled an appointment with John Ebbers, the owner of the land, to discuss the property and, of course, its price. Mr. Ebbers said he could offer Indiana Wesleyan the land for $5,000 an acre. He seemed confident with that offer, assured that we would accept because the university needed the land if it were to keep expanding. I addressed Mr. Ebbers with equal confidence, despite the fact that the university had no money and was very vulnerable to his ultimate decision. I told him I would return in a week to see if he had experienced a change of heart and wanted to help the university out of this dilemma.

I prayed along with our Administrative Council that God would help him see the importance of this acquisition to our future development. John had little knowledge of our financial situation but did understand the cause we represented. There was no plausible reason for him to lower the price for us; the price he had offered us was reasonable. But without the money in hand, we needed a miracle!

A week later, as I had promised, I returned to see John. He said he could accept $3,000 an acre. That was a 40-percent decrease in price, a total of $112,000, from his initial offer! "I will take it," I said.

I was bold in our first meeting, but now I was just presumptuous. "Now, Mr. Ebbers, can you finance the purchase?" I asked.

> God can make a way, where there seems to be no way. He works in ways we cannot see. He will make a way.
>
> —DON MOEN

We wanted to move our current athletic facilities onto the new land to allow for future academic additions to campus. Although we were making progress in paying our bills, we needed to have funds available to build additional facilities on campus. These would serve our students and make the campus attractive to prospective students and their parents. I asked Mr. Ebbers if he would consider loaning us the money to purchase his land at an interest rate that was more favorable than any bank was offering. Surprisingly, he agreed to that request, too. God was most definitely at work in this man who had no logical reason to be doing this for us.

After buying the 56 acres, we went to work putting them all to good use. Along with our loan from John, the land enabled us to move our men's and women's baseball and softball fields, track, soccer and practice fields to the new property. By freeing the land formerly used by the athletic fields, we had space to build the Phillippe Performing Arts Center, a president's home, and to renovate and triple the size of Luckey Center, our basketball arena and physical education building. Those buildings form a large part of our students' campus experiences.

I often gaze out of my office window across the campus landscape and wonder what it would look like today if God had not worked in Mr. Ebbers as He so earnestly had.

The growing landscape had the same effect on Mr. Ebbers. Not only was he proud to be part of helping Indiana Wesleyan to become the fastest-growing college in Indiana, he also was inspired to give more of his resources to the university. At the one-year mark, when the first payment was sent, Mr. Ebbers came to my office with a proposition of his own. "I want to give half of the interest on the loan payments back to the university," he said. "I want to see the university continue to grow."

God's presence in our relationship with Mr. Ebbers was undeniable. He had made a path for Indiana Wesleyan's development where previously his focus was the bottom line. Through God's boldness and God's working in his life, he was an incredibly generous man.

When you embrace God's strength of character, you can have the ability to take people who are in no way involved with your institution or your cause (and really have no reason to be), and bend their hearts in your direction. **God can ignite a great passion for your cause in potential donors' hearts.** Mr. Ebbers would never have offered Indiana Wesleyan the land if I had not asked. Nor would he have lowered the price if I had not given God time to work on his initial offer. Nor would he have offered to donate the interest money to us without any nudging at all (except a nudge from God, of course).

Still, we must remember that Christ-like boldness alone cannot yield success. It must be coupled with all of His character, and ultimately, His will. Our intentions must be to serve as the earthly conduits for His heavenly plans.

KEY TAKEAWAYS:

- As Christian fundraisers, humility is in our job description. If we are going to be successful in our pursuits, we must humble ourselves to both God and our potential donors.
- We must take the opportunities that God puts before us, even if some hurt our pride or make us uncomfortable. God has a plan.
- We should have holy boldness, trusting in God wholeheartedly. In our appeals, we can be unwavering because our strength is in God.
- Christian fundraisers must understand that to most people, money is personal. For that reason, requests for larger donations should always be made in person, with consideration for each donor's unique concerns.

CHAPTER 2

REACHING
OUT

IN THIS CHAPTER
- Prominent community figures can lend influence to your cause
- Creating interest with those not related to your organization
- Should you seek non-Christian donors as a Christian institution?
- Why a donor's lifestyle does not predict his or her gift

Asking people for money — be they family, friends or strangers — is never easy. The task requires a great deal of humility and confidence: Humility about yourself, confidence in God. Trust in Him, and you will be astounded by all of the opportunities He puts along your way. Many opportunities are the least expected ones. But while God gives us these opportunities, we must in turn recognize them — and seize them! God rewards those who strive to do His work, not those who shy away from action. We must take some steps ourselves and know that God is there to help carry us along.

. . . TO FIGURES WHO SHARE YOUR VISION

I met Tony Dungy, head coach of the Indianapolis Colts, when I scheduled him to speak at a dinner for our adult and professional students at the Columbia Club in Indianapolis. Since I had made the contact, I sat next to Tony at the event. We had a wonderful conversation about our families and work. He was very congenial and, at the end of the night, suggested that we get together again.

"Are you serious?" The question slipped from between my lips, because I had not expected that type of response. Coach Dungy assured me that he was, in fact, serious.

A few weeks later, I called to ask if he would allow me to auction a dinner with him as part of our annual telesale. I assured him that I would be the dinner's "third-wheel" of sorts to make certain everything went well. To my surprise, he agreed. He was eager to promote our mission to provide young adults with a Christian education. Dungy is a man who strives to foster a Christian atmosphere among his often-young adult players, praying for them before every game and serving as a mentor to them all year. Apparently, our interests were aligned. I invited eight to 10 people to the dinner, all of them faithful donors to Indiana Wesleyan. Everyone had a delightful evening. The dinner was very informal, and each person had the opportunity to speak with Coach Dungy and have a football autographed. (I provided the footballs.) At the conclusion of the evening, Coach Dungy reaffirmed that I could make the dinner an annual event.

We continued this for the next few years, and with each year I felt I had a better understanding of Coach Dungy and his zeal to reach people for God's Kingdom. In 2007, I invited 15 couples to the dinner so that the ladies could experience more than the Sunday afternoon National Football League sensation around the television set. The women had an opportunity to ask questions and meet a person who not only loves the game of football but also loves family and Christ.

Special paintings of Coach Dungy produced by Ron Mazellan, an illustration artist at IWU, were also given to the attendees in addition to the traditional autographed footballs. Coach Dungy was presented with his own copy of the painting as well.

During this meeting, IWU President Dr. Henry Smith, asked Coach Dungy if he would be willing to come to campus to receive the World Changer Award in recognition of his support of our university's mission to provide a strong Christian education. Past award recipients included Dr. James Dobson, Founder of Focus on the Family; best-selling Christian author, Frank Peretti; Emmy Award-winning sports executive, Bob Briner, and Dr. Ben Carson, a world-renowned pediatric surgeon at Johns Hopkins Medical Institutions.

Coach Dungy agreed to receive the award and came to campus in February of 2008. Standing before the student body at the convocation, the coach also received an honorary doctorate from Indiana Wesleyan University.

Our relationship with Coach Dungy was a wonderful opportunity for the school to gain recognition throughout the state and encourage interest in our current and potential donors. Well-known Christian figures can prove to be incredibly beneficial both as donors and as strategic partners in advancing a common goal, which in our case is reaching out to young adults for Christ.

. . . TO LIKE-MINDED CORPORATIONS

There's a risk in working for an institution whose focus is on helping people. Since Indiana Wesleyan University's inception in 1920, it has produced invaluable citizens — many of whom work in the helping professions. These include teachers, preachers, social workers, etc. Their big hearts have dictated generous giving, despite their limited incomes. Although that means much emotionally, the needs of a growing organization make it necessary to look beyond the alumni base. Jesus rejoices over all gifts, but expects us to be faithful in expanding our influence and donor base.

So, we decided to look for more money outside of our alumni base. In our town we had a Hobby Lobby store that closed on Sunday, as all of the company's stores do. Hobby Lobby owner, David Green, is a strong Christian who supports Christian causes. I called and requested an audience with Mr. Green at his Oklahoma City office, and he agreed to see me.

When I arrived at the headquarters, I was impressed by the beautiful facility. It seemed to stretch for miles. I meekly gave my name to the receptionist, and then paced eagerly around the front hall — all in view of the receptionist, of course. In the hall, a variety of wall hangings spoke to the corporation's Christian philosophy. Each represented a scene that we celebrate as part of the Christian holidays. While I was walking around, a man approached me and introduced himself as Dave Green. He ushered me into a boardroom and allowed me to speak about IWU and what we were trying to accomplish. I also had an opportunity to share what Christ was doing in my life. I will never forget his comment: "If you keep clean hands and a pure heart, God will honor and bless your organization."

After this initial encounter, I met with Dave on other trips I made to the West. After a couple of visits, I received the blessing from the University president to ask Dave to speak for our graduation ceremony. He listened to my request but assured me he was not the guy for the job. He said he was by no means a speaker. I told him that we admired his love for Christ. That made him the perfect guy for the job. We simply wanted him to share his testimony. Later he agreed to speak at the August 1999 graduation, which was about nine months away. About six months later, while visiting with Dave, he again mentioned that speaking was not his forte. In fact, he said he would give IWU "a substantial gift" in exchange for not speaking. I assured him that he needed to share his testimony and that he only had to talk for 12 minutes. Dave spoke at the commencement ceremony and did an excellent job. As I sat there with my fellow faculty members and administrators, I was proud to be listening to Dave's message. None of the well-educated faculty members suspected that Dave only had a high school education. His wisdom extended far beyond his formal training. His wisdom is something I strive for in my own life.

As is our practice at IWU, speakers at the ceremony receive an honorary doctorate. This is both an honor to the speaker and a great way for the speaker to remember the organization. It was also during this visit that the president was able to spend time with the Green family, and I was able to give them a campus tour.

Obviously, as a fundraiser, you continue to think about what the school could do with the " substantial gift " such as the one Dave offered to give to avoid speaking. But with persistence and focus I declined Dave's initial offer. And, in turn, we were able to create a far greater relationship with the Green family.

On a subsequent visit, I asked Dave if he would consider becoming a board member at IWU. He suggested that I make the offer to his wife, who sat as a board member of the multi-million-dollar Hobby Lobby Corporation. We arranged to meet with Barb to explore the possibility of her becoming a board member at IWU. She was very gracious and said that she would pray about the offer.

I also had the opportunity to meet the couple's sons, Mart and Steven. While visiting with Mart I found that he had a son, Tyler, who was a senior in high school. I began to recruit Tyler, via his father, as a potential IWU student. I shared the IWU story and the great Christian environment that his son would be nurtured in during his college career. To my surprise, during the summer of Tyler's senior year in high school, I received a telephone call from Mart saying that they were flying from Africa to Indianapolis so Tyler could take a look at IWU. This visit was an answer to prayer. We met Mart and Tyler and gave them the grand tour of campus. A few months later, Tyler registered for his freshman year at IWU.

During another visit with Barb Green, I reaffirmed our interest in her becoming a board member. She said if Tyler returned to IWU for his sophomore year she would accept the offer. Obviously, I was praying that Tyler would return. Thankfully, a few months later I saw that Tyler had registered for his sophomore year. Within a short time, Barb attended her first board meeting.

Recently I had the opportunity to attend the wedding of Tyler and his new bride, Kristin (both are alumni of IWU). As I watched the couple exchange their vows, I was moved by their deep commitment to Christ and one another. I wondered what his life would have been like if he had not attended IWU. I never imagined how his decision to attend IWU and his ensuing college years would so enrich his life.

We joked with Tyler as we went through the receiving line that I should take credit for putting the couple together since I had so heavily recruited Tyler. Tyler also mentioned that his grandfather was taking credit since he had come to IWU to speak many years ago and this was their first exposure to campus. Despite our jests, it is not about who gets the credit, but how our lives are changed by the people we meet as we are following His will for our lives. It took us years to gain the involvement we now have from the Green family. But, we were faithful and persistent, and our institution has benefitted because of it. I pray others will show the same diligence in recruiting quality people for their organizations.

. . . TO GAINING SPECIALIST INSIGHT

Herb Rickert, as mentioned earlier concerning our Grandparents Day, taught me humility when asking for gifts from potential donors. He also showed me that everyday folks can be just as beneficial to any institution as many corporate professionals can be with their business knowledge.

Around the time that Herb made his second donation, we were looking for individuals to serve on our PACE (President's Advisory Council on Excellence) group and offer expertise to our board in the area of construction. The reality was that the university was constantly in building mode. To have individuals like Herb with an understanding of construction was a blessing. PACE was created to add expertise to the Board of Trustees and to provide financial support to the University. There was no requirement of the group to represent The Wesleyan Church (which owns Indiana

Wesleyan), so that allowed us to seek a diverse membership, which came to include Herb.

Herb is a retired owner of a construction business and has provided valuable insight into our operations at IWU, which has invested more than $250 million in new buildings in recent years. As a member of our construction committee, Herb interviews prospective construction managers, architects, and other construction-related personnel.

What involvement came from my simple request for scholarship fund donations on that Grandparents Day! As administrators of formal not-for-profit institutions, we tend to seek out the advice of professionals. But, it has been my experience that by paying attention to the farmers, shopkeepers, and construction workers, you can expand your vision much further than previously imagined.

. . . TO THOSE NOT RELATED TO YOUR CAUSE

As fundraisers, we spend our days reaching out to, and cultivating relationships with, people involved with and related to our causes. We make lists upon lists of prospects until our fingers blister. Pastors reach out to their congregations, universities to their alumni. It does make perfect sense. After all, who is more apt to give than someone intimately tied with your vision and cause? While this is ultimately true, we must never discount or ignore those people who know nothing of that vision and passion. They are opportunities-in-waiting. Just because a person is not involved in, or even knows of your organization does not mean he or she cannot learn about it — or even give to it.

I've learned this lesson frequently enough that I should no longer be surprised to learn it all over. But still, God's work in these cases does not cease to astound me. This was perhaps most true in my association with Lee Beard.

During my first year at Indiana Wesleyan, a gentleman in his 80s came into my office. Standing in front of my desk, he simply said, "I would like

The Lord does not look at the things man looks at. Man looks at the outward appearance, but the LORD looks at the heart.

—1 SAMUEL 16:7

to make a donation of General Electric stock to the art department."

After some discussion, we realized that this stock was worth $670,000. Although his proposed gift was both generous and needed, I was most taken with its unusual circumstances. Lee Beard had no affiliation with the university or the Wesleyan denomination. Many questions rushed into my head. So I began to question him. *Why this gift? Do you want to direct the sum to a particular purpose within the art department? Can you afford to make this gift without jeopardizing your lifestyle or financial security?* Although not appreciating my line of questioning, he tolerated it, and after hearing his answers, I accepted his gift.

Lee Beard was a retired engineer with General Electric Corporation. He had met the chairperson of the school's art department, Professor Ardelia Williams, and the two had become friends. Since Lee was an excellent wood worker with a fully equipped shop in his home, Professor Williams had asked him to reproduce some broken parts for art department looms. Lee was fascinated with the loom and began repairing parts as they would break. Most of his work consisted of turning spindles and reproducing threads. His work was largely done on a lathe in his basement woodworking shop. Most of the parts were replaced because of age or wetness that had resulted from leaks in the basement of the old Teter Hall, where the art department had been located for many years.

The looms produced beautiful, lush fabrics for wearing, and decorative items for wall hangings and rugs. The parts that Lee reproduced had to be done with precision. The looms now functioned with precision. Lee always wanted to learn new things, and so he became familiar with looms while taking a weaving class.

With each repair and each class, Lee became more interested in Indiana Wesleyan. In fact, when he discovered that General Electric would match contributions from alumni members up to $15,000 each year, he enrolled in an art class and became an alumnus of the university.

Since the art department was operating in an inadequate building that was more than 100 years old, Lee began to suggest that IWU needed a new facility. Lee ultimately provided $3.2 million to build the university's new art facility, which now stands in the shadow of our oldest building on campus, the John Wesley Administration Building. The brass letters on the new building read: *Lee and Edna Beard Art Center, honoring Ardelia Williams, Associate Professor of Art, 1992.*

Some time later, I learned from Professor Williams that Lee accepted Christ during one of her visits to his nursing home in his final days. The visit included several members of the art department, who by now had formed an intimate friendship with Lee. I recalled a dinner where he said that we did not need to bless the food on his account. But then, before his passing he had accepted Christ into his heart. What a time of rejoicing! There was no better gift than the gift of eternal life that the faculty could help give Lee for all of his kindness to the art department.

We rejoice with all donors who make gifts that enhance the Kingdom, but it is rewarding to know that some accept Christ as their personal savior because of their gifts.

As a fundraiser, surprises such as Lee Beard enter your office in a myriad of ways. Sometimes the person from whom you are seeking a gift winds up not giving but, instead, provides the name of an unexpected, and even unknown, donor. That was the case with Jack Holmes.

A potential donor had decided that he would be unable to give IWU a donation but gracefully told us to contact his acquaintance, Jack Holmes, who might have an interest in our University. I called Jack and scheduled a luncheon in downtown Indianapolis. Other than his name, I knew nothing of the man I was about to meet.

During our first visit, I learned that Jack became an insurance agent with Northwestern Mutual, an insurance agency that had been founded and developed with his father, after Jack had served in the Armed Forces.

I shared stories of my father who was stationed in Italy during World War II, and Jack and I soon developed a genial rapport. After we chatted for about an hour, I learned that this 80-something-year-old alumnus of Indiana University had a passion for business ethics.

> Character may almost be called the most effective means of persuasion.
>
> —ARISTOTLE

Jack wanted to start a business ethics program that could be instituted at numerous universities and then adapted for kindergarten through 12th- grade students. After visiting several universities, he learned that not only did many not include business ethics across their curricula, but they also were not interested in his approach to the program. Tucked in the file cabinets of his mind, the months of research he had conducted were unloaded on me.

Business ethics: "What an important value to teach our students," I thought. "If students in all of our departments, not just business, were coached on business ethics, how much they could gain." I immediately got to work on making it happen, discussing with Indiana Wesleyan's business department how Jack's interest could dovetail with our university. We conducted an administration-wide discussion forum where Jack could express his views on business ethics with key members of the faculty. It quickly became apparent that if we launched the program at Indiana Wesleyan, we would need to get Jack thinking of the relationship between business ethics and Christian ethics. Where did they align? Where did they diverge?

We continued to define and redefine what the business ethics program would entail, and eventually landed on a model for implementing the program that was satisfactory to everyone. It was a long, tiring process, but not without its benefits. During one of our frequent meetings at a Golden Corral restaurant (Jack's favorite meeting place), he told me he was going to request that Indiana University, his alma mater, transfer about $26,000 to Indiana Wesleyan to get our business ethics program started. Within a couple of weeks, the money arrived.

Later, Jack came to a luncheon and said, "Terry, you cost me $360 today in attorney fees!"

SOCIETY OF WORLD CHANGERS

Coach Dungy received Honorary Doctorate
from IWU as part of the Society of
World Changers' ceremony.

Lyle Reed and wife, Nell, provided funds for
the Society of World Changers.

Author Frank Peretti and wife, Barbara,
at Society of World Changers' banquet.

Joni Eareckson Tada with Terry Munday
and wife, Linda

CELEBRITIES OF INFLUENCE

Gale Sayers, NFL great, practicing his putting at Jack Colescott Golf Tournament.

Coach Dungy and Terry Munday with presentation of Ron Mazellan's illustration of Super Bowl Champion Colts.

Coach Dungy with the Mundays at St. Elmo's Steak House dinner.

Dr. Memory, Jerry Lucas, participates and serves as a speaker in golf tournaments.

CELEBRITIES OF INFLUENCE

Coach Dungy signing footballs at dinner with friends.

Coach Dungy at a luncheon with Terry Munday.

Clark Kellogg speaks at the Jack Colescott Golf Tournament. Also, pictured Jack Colescott, Dave Colescott, and Glen Heaton

Mayor Wayne Seybold presents keys to the City of Marion at Jack Colescott Golf Tournament.

CELEBRITIES OF INFLUENCE

Bob VanKampen with President Barnes at graduation
and receiving of Honorary Doctorate.

Colts Coach Jim Caldwell at a dinner
with Terry Munday.

Jack Colescott, teacher, athletic
director, and coach at Marion High
School. In 2009, IWU will
celebrate the 20th year for the
Jack Colescott Golf Tournament
raising more than $900,000

Senator Evan Bayh greets students on campus.

SCHOLARSHIPS FOR STUDENTS

Tom Stone and wife, Joyce, fishing
at Isle Royale. The Stones provided
a unitrust for IWU.

Ken and Marceil Bostic sharing
a scholarship banquet on campus.

Van and Suzanne Gurley honor Roy and
Nina Trump by providing a student
scholarship in their honor.

Art Hodson at student
scholarship luncheon.

ADVANCEMENT & FUNDRAISING ACTIVITIES

Terry Munday raising money
at Chaparral with senior citizens.

Gene Beltz, Shadeland Dodge,
provided the President with
a new car each year for 19 years.

Terry Munday and wife, Linda, host a
Caribbean Cruise with alumni.

Lunch with Howard Noggle and Dan Metz
at Scholarship Luncheon. Dr. Noggle served
65 years in University Advancement.

Donor from Cedar Rapids, Iowa,
provides Hummer.

Staff celebrates the first year IWU breaks
$1 million in the Annual Fund.

ADVANCEMENT & FUNDRAISING ACTIVITIES

Indiana Pacer Clark Kellogg signs basketball to auction at Jack Colescott Golf Tournament.

Terry Munday auctions a football signed by the Indianapolis Colts for $1,000.

TELESALE ANTICS

Selling Hair Salon Gift Certificate

Selling Oreck Sweeper

Live Entertainment

Luggage to go

THE TERRY MUNDAY FAMILY

NAMING OPPORTUNITIES

Dr. Violet Jackson named the Jackson Library
in memory of her husband, Dr. Lewis Jackson,
who was a Tuskegee Airman and president
of Central State University in Ohio.

Art Hodson speaks at the naming
of Hodson Hall.

I looked at him, bewildered. He reached into his suit coat pocket and pulled out a codicil of his will. He had visited his estate planner that day and had Indiana Wesleyan included in his will. He had written the university down for $750,000. He reaffirmed his appreciation of our efforts in launching the new business ethics program. We had made his dream a reality. This was his "thank you."

Only a few weeks later, he called me, and with a troubled voice said, "Terry, I need to meet with you on Monday. Are you available?" He told me that he had made a trip to speak with an organization to discuss a gift he wanted to make and the representatives had not given him the time of day. He was deeply hurt by the treatment, which caused him to appreciate even more his relationship with us. He proceeded to tell me that he was going to add another major gift to his estate plan for IWU.

. . . TO THOSE OF DIFFERENT FAITHS

Once it makes sense to reach out to people who aren't involved in your organization, you are bound to start considering reaching outside of your faith. For some Christian institutions, this idea is quickly dismissed. But from my experience, non-Christian donors can be great assets to Christian causes.

Take Adam Ray, for instance. He was a man with a perfect Biblical name, but I don't know if he ever had put forth any study of the Good Book. Our annual scholarship telesale was the event that first brought Adam and me together. Adam had seen me requesting money during the annual TV auction and, after three years, he wanted to see the production live so he made his way to the university's Phillippe Performing Arts Center. After completing one of my familiar stage antics, I saw someone motioning for me to come to the front of the stage. I tentatively walked up to the man, hoping I hadn't done something to offend him. That is when I first met Adam. Fortunately, I hadn't done anything to offend him. He wanted to talk to me about IWU. We chatted for a few minutes and decided we would meet a few days later for breakfast and to talk about the University.

I learned over those first plates of bacon and eggs and mugs of coffee that Adam had been a tool and die worker at the local RCA-Thomson Consumer Electronics plant until his retirement a few years earlier. To earn some extra income while staying busy and traveling (a large passion of his), he now drove cars — locally as well as out-of-state — as far away as California, Arizona, and Ohio for a local auto dealer. He earned $5 an hour, but the money wasn't important. Adam just wanted something to do.

We talked about the growing student population at Indiana Wesleyan University, and the need for housing and other facilities for the students. Adam was not familiar with university life other than his limited exposure in the local community. I told him how we worked to raise scholarship money so that every student who wished to fulfill his or her education at the university could afford to do so. He was definitely interested in what we were doing, but I did not immediately know why. He had lived in the Grant County community all of his life, but was neither college-educated nor a man who claimed to know Christ. He was practical, in a sense, and faith did not factor into his practicality.

. . . TO THOSE OF HUMBLE LIVES

The fact that a non-Christian man had actively sought me to explore the possibilities of donating to Indiana Wesleyan was staggering, and I appreciated his generosity and kindness of heart. Judging from his former and current jobs, as well as by his simple dress, I didn't expect much from Adam, dollar-wise at least. I thought $1,000 might be a stretch. But I remembered the words of Luke 21:1-4 (NKJV): "And He looked up and saw the rich putting their gifts into the treasury, and He saw also a certain poor widow putting in two mites. So He said, 'Truly I say to you that this poor widow has put in more than all; for all these out of their abundance have put in offerings for God, but she out of her poverty put in all the livelihood that she had.'" God would indeed rejoice in Adam's gift as well.

> The world asks, "What does a man own?" Christ asks, "How does he use it?"
>
> —ANDREW MURRAY

Still, my estimate of his possible gift dropped even lower when I visited Debbie, his long-time companion, at the home they shared. Although Adam was hesitant for people to visit (I soon understood why), I had occasion to be in his home after a few months. The interior of the two-story, brick home was stained with water leaks that had dripped from the ceiling. The floor was 4x8-foot pieces of plywood, rubbed down from years of use. Pieces of cloth were pinned over the windows. Curtains were yet another luxury that Adam did not need. Bed sheets covered the couches where Adam relaxed while watching his favorite sports teams on TV.

But I soon learned that appearances don't mean much when it comes to giving and wealth. And sometimes, neither does logic. Giving simply works out as God has intended.

A few months after that first visit, Adam met with our director of estate planning, Ross Hoffman, to see what estate plan would best serve his and Debbie's needs and interests. Another example of Adam's frugality came as the estate planning process unfolded. Adam was told that he could save another $675,000 in taxes if he and Debbie got married. They had lived together for nearly 40 years, but Adam had never taken the time to complete the wedding vows. Now, without hesitation, Adam agreed to get married and off to the justice of the peace they went. Ross stood with the couple as their witness.

Adam later decided on a gift of $3.5 million to Indiana Wesleyan. The money was used to assist in the construction of a new residence facility on campus.

I had a similarly surprising experience with Bruce and Dorothy Cox. Bruce was an attorney in Michigan, and Dorothy was the daughter of a missionary. They had three sons. Bruce had been a member of the university's

Board of Trustees for many years, and one of his sons had continued his father's legacy by serving with our PACE group.

Almost every year, President Dr. Jim Barnes and I traveled to Florida, although sometimes I made the long trip by myself. In the early years, we would stay in homes to keep our travel costs to a minimum and, in many cases, would have meals in the homes of donors or prospective donors. It provided us a great chance to bond with our snowbird friends. We would go to bed with a smile and get up the next morning with an equally big smile — even though our backs ached from sleeping on different mattresses. That was the price we paid for staying in homes. But don't get me wrong; our hosts were always tremendously gracious and kind. We could always count on Bruce and Dorothy to open their Florida home to us.

When we arrived at their home, we would generally find Bruce picking up sticks to keep the fireplace going, or Dorothy on a stepladder five feet in the air, retrieving oranges from their trees to tide us over in our travels. (Keep in mind that these two were in their 80's.) They were simple people with generous hearts. In addition to gaining their good company, we almost always left with a $25,000 check for the University.

Bruce and Dorothy would never allow us to take them out to eat. They felt that if we did, we would be spending money that could be better used to serve our students. They were always thinking of others.

On one occasion, Dorothy offered to fix me a meal and told me where I could wash my hands. As soon as I entered the bathroom, I noticed soapy, milky-colored water in the bathtub. I proceeded to use the restroom and flushed the toilet. To my surprise, I witnessed red, rusty water gush into the toilet bowl from the water closet.

When I returned to the kitchen, Dorothy smiled and said, "You flushed the toilet."

I apologetically asked, "I wasn't supposed to?"

"Oh, yes. But I forgot to tell you about our 'practice.' We dip our bath water from the tub into the toilet to flush it" (which explained both the milky water and the rust). She explained that it kept the pump from running, which saved both electricity and money.

I thought, *My wife thinks I'm fiscally conservative now... Just wait until I introduce this 'practice' at home!*

I then realized why I had so often seen Bruce collecting branches for the fireplace. It saved their heating costs.

Here was a couple who practiced Christian stewardship to the maximum degree. They were willing to give up conveniences to provide scholarship funds to deserving students. Although some may say their "practices" were overboard in trying to save money, I believe one must look upon the heart and not the lifestyle.

When Bruce and Dorothy Cox died, they gave more than $2.7 million to three universities, including Indiana Wesleyan. That was in addition to the hundreds of thousands of dollars they had given to those same universities throughout their lifetime.

As Randy Alcorn writes of the treasure principle, "You can't take it with you — but you *can* send it on ahead."[1] This is what the Coxes were really practicing. They preferred to invest in their eternal futures above their own worldly comfort. They saw the value in what we were working to accomplish at IWU and knew that it was part of His ultimate plan. Rich will be their reward in Heaven.

KEY TAKEAWAYS:

- Well-known Christian figures can prove to be incredibly beneficial both as donors and as strategic partners in advancing a common goal.
- Seeking financial help from like-minded corporations can give a big boost to a nonprofit organization.
- Involvement can also be a great form of a donation. For IWU, donor participation on our Board of Trustees and PACE group has been incredibly fruitful.

- Just because someone hasn't been related to your cause doesn't mean they can't be in the future. Never pigeonhole someone as never being interested. Everyone is a potential donor.
- God rejoices in any gift, however big or small. The real gift is from the heart, not from the wallet.

CHAPTER 3

PERSISTENCE PAYS OFF

IN THIS CHAPTER
- The importance of following leads
- Never give up on a donor

"Persistence pays off." Like most clichés, this one is true. For fundraisers, this phrase actually can be quite literal. Big persistence. Big gains.

PURSUING LEADS

During a university function, one of our alumni pastors pulled me aside to tell me that Lyle Reed, a former member of his church, had been a successful railroad entrepreneur and had sold his business for several million dollars. Think of the opportunity for Christian stewardship. Our alumnus went on to say that Lyle would make an excellent member for Indiana Wesleyan's Board of Trustees or PACE group. Although the pastor had given leads such as this to other organizations, he later told me that those organizations had failed to follow up on them.

I assured him I would not add IWU to that list. The prospective donor would be hearing from me soon. The lead was like music to my well-tuned ears, so when I planned my next trip West, I included a stop in Dallas where Lyle lived. I called to schedule a dinner with him and his wife, Nell. I explained to Lyle that his former pastor had given me his name, and I wanted to meet him and his wife. They were more than willing to meet, and they turned out to be just about the nicest people I had ever met. They were easy to talk with, and their interests paralleled the interests of the University. Lyle and Nell deeply loved Christ and the Church.

I invited them to come to Marion and visit our campus. Without hesitation, they agreed, and after the visit I asked Lyle if he would consider joining our PACE group and then moving to the Board of Trustees when there was a vacant seat. After some prayer, he agreed and became a valuable asset to the leadership team. Within four years, he was elected as chairman of the Board of Trustees.

> Every success is usually an admission ticket to a new set of decisions.
>
> —HENRY KISSINGER

Soon after Lyle began his tenure with the university, we made plans to approach him with a capital campaign request. About that time, the Reeds invited my wife and me to join them in Branson, Missouri, for a three-day vacation. Their hospitality was incredible. A couple of days into the trip, Lyle asked if we would be interested in a gift from his trust. I am known for accepting a gift in most any form and size, and his was no exception. The gift turned out to be $1 million.

Lyle and Nell later provided the initiative — and the funding — to establish the annual Indiana Wesleyan World Changers Award. The award is given to a figure of national prominence who has served as salt and light to the world. The award makes clear to our student body that they, too, can become world changers in their own right. Often the recipients have come from humble beginnings and have followed God's leading, preparing themselves academically to influence the world for good. By providing $100,000 to jumpstart the fund, the Reeds created a venue for our students to connect with such distinguished Christians as Coach Tony Dungy. Each year, it is a great joy to watch as these World Changers come to campus to challenge our students with their walks of faith.

In conversation with the Reeds over the years, I have asked them why they chose to give away their money and why they elected to do their estate planning early in life. They said that the gifts express their priorities, and they didn't want to leave that responsibility for someone else to decide. "We are able to witness the use of the gifts during our lifetime," the Reeds said. What a wonderful testimony of giving and receiving the benefit during our time on earth.

On another occasion, I received a telephone call from a Christian organization that was struggling to meet its annual expenses. The organization needed an idea to help raise funds quickly. Since John Maxwell is a personal friend and has a national reputation as a leadership authority, I asked him if he would do a half-day seminar at no cost to the requesting organization. He agreed, and we decided to host a 30-person roundtable event for $2,500 each. I made several successful calls on area business people and, after exhausting my leads with people who had a link with the organization, I still needed to sell a few more seats. I asked the development director for names of people in the area who either had a heart for the community or who had a reputation of generosity. The development director identified an individual in the community who did a lot of advertising and gave to many worthwhile charitable causes. His name was John Pierson, the owner of a Toyota dealership in the community. I then asked the development director to accompany me on those calls, since my background of the organization was limited.

The one thing I did have to offer was the intestinal fortitude to try to get us an audience with people who had little or no experience with the organization. The director said he understood that it was not easy to get an audience with John Pierson, but I still wanted to try—even at the risk of being turned away by a secretary or other employee of the dealership.

As we drove into the dealership, every parking space was filled, but one of the employees signaled for us to pull into the handicap spot, and we followed his instructions. What the employee didn't know was that we really were handicapped in our effort to meet with the owner of the dealership.

"What can I do for you?" the employee asked us. I immediately said we were there to see John Pierson. He indicated that we should follow him through the front door, across the large showroom floor, and back to an office in the rear of the building. I seem to thrive on these types of situations, while the development director followed with amazement.

At the office window, we were asked who we wanted to see. "John Pierson", I said.

"Do you have an appointment?" The receptionist responded.

"No, but we have an idea that we think Mr. Pierson will be very interested in," I replied.

"Who do you represent?" In an effort not to receive an immediate rejection, I said, "John Maxwell. He is a leading authority on leadership in the U.S." I thought that John Pierson might have read one of Maxwell's books and that might intrigue him enough that he would agree to see us. I also hoped that my boldness would be a good lesson for the development director on how to break down walls or barriers.

At that point, the receptionist referred me to John's secretary, who was on the second floor, and said that we could take the elevator. We followed her instructions and exited the elevator on the second floor to meet John's secretary, who told us that John was busy and was not taking appointments. I assured her that I only needed a few minutes and would not monopolize John's time. In fact, we could just make it a standup meeting. She left and within a short time a tall, slender man appeared at the doorway. He introduced himself as John Pierson.

"Thank you for seeing us!" I told him. "We will not take much of your time. My name is Terry Munday, and I am representing this organization that is bringing John Maxwell to your area for a roundtable presentation."

"My son's name is John Maxwell," he said. "Come on in and have a seat." Here I am thinking that John Pierson might agree to see us because he's familiar with John Maxwell, the author, but instead I'm now learning that he is intrigued because his son has a similar name. *Wait until I tell this story to John Maxwell*, I told myself!

For the next 45 minutes, we told John Pierson about our upcoming event and how we needed his participation. I suggested that he go online and check out both John Maxwell and me. He shared that he would and that he had an interest in helping us. I assured him that I would call him in a week to determine his interest in the project.

A few days later, I met with John Maxwell to confirm his roundtable seminar and the logistics that would be involved. Maxwell had just completed his new book, *Leadership Gold*, and had a signed copy for me. I shared my story about John Maxwell Pierson, and John Maxwell chuckled and signed another copy of the book for John Pierson. In the book, John wrote, "To John Pierson, I hope to see you at our upcoming roundtable."

As I drove away, I decided I would deliver the book to John Pierson at the dealership. I proceeded to the window in the back of the dealership and again asked to see John. I then went through the series of questions again. Again, I was permitted to go up the elevator and meet John's secretary. She once again said that John was very busy, and I assured her that I simply wanted to give a book to John that had been signed by John Maxwell. She disappeared and within a few moments John Pierson appeared at the door. He accepted the book and said that he had checked out John Maxwell and me and that he would sponsor two seats for the seminar. That was a gift of $5,000. I insisted that John use one of the seats himself, and he assured me that he would.

Needless to say, my steps were much lighter when I left his office that day. The seminar was a great success, and John Pierson attended with a young man, Luke Murphy, an Iraqi veteran who lost a leg during the war. John Maxwell recognized him and thanked him for his service to our country. The group responded by giving Luke a standing ovation. Needless to say, the seminar was a great success and both John Pierson and Luke Murphy had a great time. John Pierson was a great lead.

> Let me tell you the secret that has led me to my goal. My strength lies solely in my tenacity.
>
> —LOUIS PASTEUR

Oftentimes, we think that "high walls" exist, and sometimes they do, but we must exercise our abilities to reach those who want to hear of our cause. Really, they are only a test of our resilience and faith in God. Just like Philippians 4:13 says, "I can do everything through him who gives me strength."

REWARDS REQUIRE DEDICATION

More than 15 years ago, I started calling on Jim Sutter. He owned several convenience stores in our community and the surrounding area. Although he dearly loved his community and was actively involved in various philanthropic organizations, we were only able to get Jim to support Indiana Wesleyan in a small way. He agreed to give us a token $200 to $500 each year as part of the annual Grant County Scholarship Day. But, we were always interested in increasing the amount. We invited him to functions on campus on a regular basis, and just as frequently received no response.

> Remember that Babe Ruth struck out 1,330 times. If we give up after a donor says "no" one time, shame on us.

However, with each phone call and visit, I continued to share the progress that we were making at Indiana Wesleyan. There were times when I could not get an audience with Jim, so I would meet with his daughter, Kelly Snyder, who was responsible for the day-to-day operations of Jim's stores. She would serve as our connection to her father.

After several visits with Jim, I learned that his brother, Jack, had attended Indiana Wesleyan at the age of 40 to seek a teaching degree after working most of his life in the family dairy business. Jack had been an extremely successful competitor against a much younger group of tennis players, earning awards during his college career while also helping the university continue its winning tradition in tennis.

Jim, who dearly loved his brother, asked what was involved in a naming opportunity on the campus. He wanted to explore naming the Indiana Wesleyan tennis courts in honor of his brother, Jack. We were excited about the naming opportunity for three reasons: First, Jack was an exemplary man. He had dedicated his life to the service of special education for young people, while still distinguishing himself as a true professional and strong Christian, not to mention a tennis champion. Second, it would be a great opportunity to get the Sutter family involved in Indiana Wesleyan. And, third, we would be able to raise money for the university to resurface its tennis courts. Hey, you have to be practical!

The naming ceremony was a great experience for the community, the Sutter family and the university. I consider it our turning point in Indiana Wesleyan's relationship with Jim and his wife, Nedra. I am convinced that our relationship grew stronger as Jim began to realize the importance of Indiana Wesleyan to so many people.

Jim soon became a member of our PACE group, sharing his business expertise and becoming more involved with the University.

When Jim sold his string of Handy Andy Stores, I immediately called on him. Little did I know that the day we met was the very day that the transaction was completed on his stores and the money was transferred into his bank account. Jim probably thought I had an inside track, but God's timing is perfect.

During our visit, Jim asked me what I wanted as a gift. That was a new one for me. Normally, I made the ask and waited for the response. "Tell me the amount you want me to give," Jim said.

I looked at him and asked for $250,000. "You got it," he said.

Although we spent many years cultivating our relationship with Jim, and waiting for God's plan to take shape, we never gave up. As a Christian fundraiser, you cannot be discouraged when prospective donors are reluctant to give to your cause. As Proverbs 24:16 says, "For a righteous man falls seven times, and rises again." You must be faithful and persistent to see His will done.

KEY TAKEAWAYS:

- Networking with like-minded individuals and businesses is a great way to find promising potential donors. Never fail to ask your associates if they know of anyone who could be an asset to your organization, whether that is through a financial or time commitment.
- We must have dedication in our relationships with potential donors. It took several years to get Jim Sutter involved with IWU. But when he decided to give, it proved to be incredibly fruitful, both for the school and for him personally.
- Our perception that " high walls" or barriers exist in making successful donor calls may reflect our concern as fundraisers that we will experience failure.

PART 3

FUNDRAISING *GETS* PERSONAL

NO COW WILL LET DOWN
HER MILK IN RESPONSE TO A
LETTER OR A TELEPHONE CALL.
YOU HAVE GOT TO SIT DOWN
BESIDE HER AND GO TO WORK.

—JAMES R. REYNOLDS

CULTIVATING DONOR LOYALTY

IN THIS CHAPTER
- Using donor involvement to generate giving
- The spirit of giving catches on
- Keeping donors plugged into your institution
- The importance of building donor-recipient relationships

INVOLVEMENT ENCOURAGES GIVING

Many people — maybe even most — do not know about your organization. They do not know its mission, values or background. And they will never give to your organization without knowing something about it. For you, me, and every fundraiser, the job is making sure people do know.

For better or worse, you are the first impression that prospective donors will have of your organization. When they think of your school, charity, or institution, they will think of you. Are you trustworthy? Are you passionate about your cause? Do you care about what I have to say?

You are literally the face and voice of your cause. This isn't meant to be intimidating, but rather to give you an understanding of your role. Your job during initial meetings with potential donors is to introduce them to your cause. Give a bit of background on your organization, but don't bore them with a homily filled with facts and figures. Just give them an overview of what your organization looks like.

Then, it's time to get personal. Share stories that represent the organization's mission and values. Why is the organization needed in society? What services does it provide its beneficiaries? This may be the time to explain why you are involved, sharing the qualities of the organization that caused you to get involved. In a way you are a fast-forwarded version of your potential donor. At one time you knew nothing about the organization, and now you care about it greatly. We must present a compelling vision for our institution's ministry and mission. Countless non-profit organizations are vying for donor dollars. Why should the donor choose yours?

But talking can only do so much. That's why at Indiana Wesleyan we like to get our potential donors involved in the campus. There's no better way to make an impersonal organization or cause personal than to get people involved. In a personal survey that I conducted of the Council for Christian Colleges and Universities, I found that personal involvement is a sure-fire way to interest potential donors in giving money. Once people develop a relationship or an emotional tie with a cause, people want to see the organization thrive. Suddenly, they have a sense of ownership.

> Caring is a powerful business advantage.
>
> —Scott Johnson

I have found that one of the best ways to get prospective donors involved is to bring them to campus to meet students, faculty and staff. They need to witness the synergism of the campus community. This personal introduction will plant a seed of interest that will hopefully flourish with time and care.

After learning about the unique interests of your donor, you should plug them into a facet of your institution to which they can relate. Quality involvement should breed additional involvement — including giving. Prospective donors have a vested interest once they see the plan, which they have helped to fund, move to the point of being placed into practice.

There's no cookie-cutter mold when it comes to getting donors involved. I met many business people during my time on the IWU advancement team. As a result, we invited 25 people to serve as members of our PACE group because we knew their interest in business would offer a good transfer of learning to our institution. When they saw their ideas being implemented with an impact on the organization, they began to take ownership and increased their involvement.

The prospective donor must realize that the organization is authentic in its desire to foster involvement. We made this apparent by having the PACE members meet at the same time as our Board of Trustees. They were able to get firsthand exposure to the good, bad and ugly of our school. But, most of all, they appreciated our honesty with them. The potential donor is an insider. Although they are busy people and have many demands on their time, donors realize their lives are incomplete without involvement in a worthwhile organization that can add value to their lives. Everyone enjoys being a part of something bigger than themselves.

> Fundraising requires both optimism and realism. Without the first, few if any gift solicitation efforts would be made. Without the second, few if any would succeed.
>
> —Howard L. Jones

For example, one of our PACE members had a strong interest in financial investing, including stocks and bonds. After serving for a few months, he got involved in the investment committee and played a key role in the University's financial affairs. His interests continued to flourish until he was asked to become a member of the Board of Trustees. Now he heads the investment committee, analyzing and assisting with the school's investments. He provides the school with the same financial expertise that he does for his own personal portfolio.

An invitation to speak at an event, such as commencement, is also a great way to get potential donors involved in a meaningful way. There they can experience — and be part of — an important moment in the history of your organization. They begin to see the difference your organization is making in the bigger picture.

Sometimes to tap into potential donors' interests, you simply need to bring your organization to them. Our University Chorale, which travels across the country on behalf of IWU, is made up of between 65 and 80 students who can make sounds like no other group in the United States. People who hear them are in awe of their talent. One such gentleman, Mr. Robert Van Kampen, founder of Van Kampen Mutual Funds, heard them sing at one performance in Grand Haven, Michigan. Their music and Christian witness piqued his interest in IWU.

After hearing the Chorale, Mr. Van Kampen visited our campus for a Christmas Madrigal dinner. It was a joy to have him and his wife, Judy, on campus. Although he was suffering with some major health issues and a serious heart condition, he attended the Madrigal in high spirits.

Later, he told me he had purchased a 100-plus room castle in Herefordshire, England, in a competitive auction against Princess Diana. This was the estate of King Henry IV of England prior to his ascension to the throne. Mr. Van Kampen had spent $20 million on restoring the castle and grounds. He offered to give the Chorale $100,000 to fly to England and sing in full 18th century costume for the dedication of the castle. Needless to say, it was a great opportunity for the Chorale and a way to further cultivate our relationship with Mr. Van Kampen.

Mr. Van Kampen also owned one of the largest private collections of Biblical manuscripts in the world and went on to start the Holy Land Experience theme park in Orlando, Florida.

Our relationship was cut short when Mr. Van Kampen died suddenly while awaiting a heart transplant. Although we had hoped to further our relationship with him, it was not part of God's plan.

Over the years I have worked with many individuals who wished to promote a program at the university, but he or she passed away before making the final arrangements. Often, people who had good intentions of leaving funds to our organization procrastinated too long, and our wait ended without completing estate plans that included our organization.

That's not to say you should pressure your older potential donors. You should simply convey to them that sooner is always better than later when it comes to finalizing these plans.

A gentleman who we visited numerous times in Lost Tree Village, West Palm Beach, Florida, noted his interest in helping the school. His father, Arthur E. Rittenhouse, was credited with developing the first multi-note, bar-type door chime in the early 1900s. Lloyd Rittenhouse was another person who was drawn to us by the Chorale. He was enamored with the Chorale as they sang at the village's chapel. On one occasion, Lloyd Rittenhouse was unable to attend the concert because of health issues, but one of our staff members visited Lloyd and asked him if he would like for us to bring a music group to his home to sing. We honored his request by taking a small male ensemble to his home. He was thrilled with the effort. Sometimes you have to accommodate your prospects by going the extra mile and, yes, bring your organization to them.

We visited Mr. Rittenhouse several times, and during one of my visits to his home he indicated that he was going to include IWU in his estate plans for $100,000 to fund scholarships. I drew up an agreement and during my next visit left the scholarship agreement with him. He said that he would include the agreement in his "important paper file." Although we never received a signed agreement, upon his death I received a call from his attorney indicating that Mr. Rittenhouse's wishes were to give IWU $100,000 and that the estate was going to honor his wishes. Within a few months we received a check for $100,000.

Although very rare, the estate honored his intention even though it had not been included in his estate plans and the paperwork had not been completed. Mr. Rittenhouse conveyed his wishes to his loved ones, and he was fortunate to have a family and attorney that respected those wishes. If only our organizations could always be so blessed.

At IWU, our continued success with the donor rests in our focus and dedication to connect each donor with an individual cause. We don't hit up every donor for the campaign of the day. We ask for financial gifts, according to what the donor has a heart for. **Too often, fundraisers try to shift the donor's interest into another area — and the results can be devastating.** Many of our donors have had an interest in nursing, because they have seen the value of the profession in caring for a family member throughout an illness. We have asked for their participation in our nursing program. If we tried to steer them toward some other project, such as art or business, we would have risked losing their interest – and their support. When people have a passion for a cause, that's when they are most apt to give. We must respect the idea that our donors aren't giving away their money, they're investing in their cause.

Simple things such as asking potential donors to attend an event, to volunteer, or to give their input, are often appreciated. As long as you are making the person feel like a valued part of your organization, you are doing your job in generating interest. Involvement produces a greater commitment and fulfills a basic human need of association. In our case, people like to associate with a growing, vibrant, winning organization. There is a sense of prestige that comes to a person who is involved with that type of organization. Everyone wants to be involved in that type of organization. The best way to people's wallets is not through their back pockets, but through their hearts.

GIVING (DONE RIGHT) IS CONTAGIOUS

Larry Maxwell caught the giving bug. An astute businessman who was very successful in land development, Larry learned of the inner workings of the school and all of its benefits in students' lives through serving on our Board of Trustees. He also learned to give of himself.

After I developed a personal relationship with Larry, he suggested that the university sponsor a golf outing in Florida during the winter months.

Since Larry owned several golf courses in the Lakeland, Florida, area he offered to host a golf outing at no cost to the university. Over the next 15 years, we took Larry up on his offer, and the outing evolved into a 90-plus person event over a three-day period in the warmth of Florida. Each participant paid $2,000 for the three-day golf event. The 2005 outing was different. The rains came on Friday, when we usually hold a challenge on a par 3 hole to raise money for student scholarships. Normally, we raised between $40,000 to $100,000 on the challenge hole. With the exception of a few diehard golfers, I decided to salvage part of the day by taking the group to a recently released movie titled *End of The Spear*, which was produced by an IWU student's father, Mart Green. That was a great way to pass the time during the rains, but did little to make up for money that we generally raised on that day.

At dinner that evening, Larry had an idea. "Let's challenge these guys to give tonight," he said. "I'll triple match any gift of $2,500 or more." In addition, Lilly Endowment had one of its famous challenges going on that would add $1.50 for each $1.00 raised. Quickly we sprang into action and asked the restaurant owner if he would provide 100 sheets of paper and pens so everyone could write down a pledge. Next, I pulled a tape measure from my briefcase and used it as a prop to demonstrate the challenge. Two and a half feet represented $2,500, and with the triple match it became 10 feet, or $10,000. This provided a vivid picture of the tremendous opportunity that was before us. I made the challenge and collected the pledges to tabulate when I returned to my hotel room.

As I read the pledges one by one, I was encouraged by the response. At least until I got to the pledge that read $100,000 which, with the matching funds from Larry and Lilly Endowment, represented a gift of $1 million. At that point my heart stopped. I knew from past years that Larry was not anticipating that kind of response from our donors. How would I break this "good news" to Larry? If he matched all the pledges, he would be writing a check for $395,000. Needless to say, I didn't sleep that night. How was I going to tell my dear friend Larry that he owed IWU

$395,000? One option was to talk to the person who gave the $100,000 and ask him to reduce his gift, but that seemed counter-productive. The second option was to call Larry and tell him that I have both good news and bad news, and that was the option I chose.

The next day I called Larry to report the news. The good news, I told him, was that the golfers responded favorably to the challenge. The bad news was that he'd have to write a check for $395,000 if he wanted to follow through on the challenge. I was prepared for the worst.

"I'll pay it," he said. "That is more than I was expecting, but it is going to a good cause."

A few days later Larry flew to Marion to pay his pledge. He entered my office and handed me a check for $400,000.

"I rounded up," he laughed.

He certainly had a heart for giving. His challenge, coupled with the Lilly Endowment challenge, allowed us to raise $1,437,000 and $1,800,000 for the total golf trip that year.

KEEP YOUR DONORS IN THE KNOW

One of the most common mistakes fundraisers make is to believe the job is finished once they have the check in hand. The truth is that's really just the beginning. When potential donors become actual donors, you must realize that they have just given their *first* gift, not their *only* gift. The fruits of that gift, as well as your relationship with the donor, can lead to further involvement and blessings for both the donor and your organization.

We should never forget that no fundraising effort ever succeeds unless one person asks another person for money.

—ANDREW D. PARKER, JR.

First and foremost, show appreciation. Recognize the gift over and over by providing updates on the impact the gift is making. Stress the successes. People give to our organizations to realize a benefit. Second (and this is what must continue for the long haul) we must show an interest in them as people, not just what their money can do for our organizations.

How should you do this? Personal visits are always most appreciated, but that does not discount telephone calls, letters, birthday cards, anniversary cards, and other personal touches. Send donors updates on the organization so they feel like insiders. This will help them gain a sense of ownership in the organization and not feel like a passing fad. We must continue listening to our donors if we are going to shape another request that will catch their imagination and turn an organization's dreams into realities.

After donors make a gift to IWU, each of them receives a personal letter from me with updates on the institution and an update on my family, which many donors have come to know through my regular letters.

Introducing your donors to other members of your staff also can benefit your cause. We often use two people on an ask for two reasons. First, to make certain that the ask was made for the amount identified before the visit. Second, to expose the donor to other people on our advancement team who can relate to the donor. If donors cannot always reach you, it's good to have a second person to return calls. Even if you have an excellent friendship with the potential donor, meeting one more person will make the donor feel more valued.

The ability to think on your feet and be creative in designing a project specifically for the donor is a key attribute of a successful fundraiser. The art of listening and framing donors' wishes in a way that lets them know you care about their personal concerns can make a difference in allowing for an ongoing relationship. Whether it's a dedication of a facility in honor of a family member or helping them with their financial investments, tapping donors' needs and desires does matter.

It requires time to develop a relationship in which donors feel comfortable sharing their real needs. One of our donors, an elderly gentleman, said he always felt that a shirt and tie should be worn to church.

Unfortunately, I learned this after wearing an open-collar shirt when I went to church with him. After that, I always complied by wearing a shirt and tie when we went to church. It was a simple way to respect the feelings of the donor.

I think we have a responsibility to accommodate those who are giving to our institutions. Incidentally, this elderly gentleman has given nearly $1 million to our university. Within reason, it is best to be flexible with and to accommodate your donors. Our goal is to have a relationship and the donor's confidence at a level that will maximize the gift.

I recall asking a lady for a gift of $500,000, and her response was, "Wow, that's a lot of money." But then I suggested she look at spreading the gift over three years, which would be only $187,500 a year. Immediately she said she could do that. So, always remember, you can eat an elephant one bite at a time. Respecting the donor's needs, boundaries, and preferences will help you gain their respect in return. And maybe that respect will lead to friendship. And friendship will lead to a more substantial gift. Friendship never hurts.

DONOR-RECIPIENT RELATIONSHIPS

Why do so many nonprofit organizations send donors photos of the children, animals, or buildings that they are supporting with their dollars? Because witnessing the fruits of a donation is one sure-fire way to keep people giving.

Most often at IWU, this practice takes the form of the development team telling donors the stories of the students, departments, and programs they are supporting. But this is just the beginning.

We require our student recipients to write a letter to donors thanking them for the gift. Included in the letter are the reasons for the students' needs and why the gifts will make a difference in their lives. Often those letters tell of parents who are unemployed, or parents who refused to pay their child's way because the child chose a Christian college. Donors are answers to those kinds of prayers.

As I mentioned earlier, one donor, Brooks Fortune, doubled his gift from $10,000 to $20,000 each year after reading the letters of students who received financial assistance from his scholarship fund. He was emotional as he read the stories. We also provide donors with an annual summary of all monies expended out of their scholarship account, which adds accountability.

These personal stories give heart and meaning to the giving process. They help donors internalize the mission of the organization, while confirming their desire that the money will be used as intended. **Everyone who gives deserves to know how his or her money has been used or spent.** These letters encourage donors to consider future gifts.

Each year our advancement team has a luncheon and invites all donors who have established a scholarship fund. All scholarship recipients are invited to sit with their benefactor at the event. This face-to-face time pays huge dividends in personalizing the giving process. This is when the true mission of giving really hits home for many donors. They realize they have enriched the Kingdom of God.

> Feeling gratitude and not expressing it is like wrapping a gift and not giving it.
>
> —UNKNOWN

There are times when donors want to remain anonymous. One such couple was Herb and Donna Rickert. I told Herb that he was denying himself and his wife a blessing by not meeting with the students. With much encouragement, he decided to attend an appreciation luncheon. After the luncheon where he met the recipient of his scholarship, Herb told me how grateful he was to have attended and to have met the student he helped.

These luncheons become a blessing to both the student and the donor. Donors become partners in the success of the recipients, giving them a greater reason to pray for and with the recipients. Students and donors often establish friendships that endure for a lifetime.

KEY TAKEAWAYS:

- As fundraisers, you are the first impression that prospective donors will have of your organization. Your job is to convey the heart of your organization in your first meeting with potential donors. Show them that you care for the organization and that you care for them, too.

- Countless nonprofits are vying for donor dollars. Why should potential donors choose yours?

- When asking for a financial gift, tailor it to the interests of the potential donor. Ask yourself who will truly have a heart for the campaign at hand.

- When you receive a financial gift, show appreciation! Provide the donor with regular updates on the impact his or her gift is making at your institution. People give to an organization to realize a benefit, and they deserve to know what happens with their money.

- Keep focused on the donor. Remember donors are not giving away money; they are investing in their cause.

CHAPTER 2

—⊷⊷⊷—

INVEST *IN* POTENTIAL DONORS

IN THIS CHAPTER
- Build a personal relationship
- Invest yourself, too
- Use your abilities to the fullest

BUILD A PERSONAL RELATIONSHIP

The largest gift we ever received from an individual, $10 million, came from Art Hodson.

Art was a humble man who loved the Lord. After his first wife, Mary, died he was lonely until he met Nelle, who became the second love of his life. Nelle made Art incredibly happy, and even introduced him to a more modern wardrobe.

We later proposed naming one of our residence halls in honor of the Hodsons, and they were humbled by the offer. Soon after, the 206-bed

Fundraising is not an event; it is a process.

—EDGAR D. POWELL

residence hall became a form of ministry for the couple and for the students who lived there. It was commonplace for Art and Nelle to take students who lived in their residence hall out to eat and to build friendships with them. The students celebrated Art's 90th birthday in the residence hall. The building was much more than a place where students lived. It was a blessing for both the students and the couple.

Art and Nelle were married for almost nine years before she died. At the funeral, Art told hundred of friends, "I don't know why God took Nelle. We were having such a good life together. But God did give us almost nine wonderful years together, and I thank God for those years."

I recall spending an evening with Art at his home discussing the many blessings that he had experienced during his 90-plus years and his years with Nelle. He was incredibly strong in his faith, but the loss of Nelle hit him hard. As we prepared to go to sleep that night, Art and I made plans to go out for breakfast the next morning. About 1:30 a.m., Art came into my bedroom. He was fully dressed, including suit and tie, and ready for breakfast. He had, of course, misread the clock. I got out of bed to assure Art that we would go in five hours. He spent the rest of that night on his recliner fully dressed.

It was my privilege as Art's friend to be there for him during some difficult times. After his passing, I knew that the advancement staff had done right by him, and that his life was blessed by both IWU and our friendship. His friendship blessed me as well.

When we recognize that a better word for fundraising is "friend raising," we open limiless doors to creativity in support of our causes.

—SUE VINEYARD

Being a friend to donors does not mean following any to-do list of favors. More than anything, friendship is caring and expressing that care for others. If we love others as God loves us, friendship will follow everywhere we go.

Here is another example of expressing our love to others.

Every couple of weeks, I drove to the home of Vance and Eileen Jett, where I was always received with a warm smile. The two sisters lived on a 100-acre farm just outside of Marion. Neither of them had ever married, and they lived a humble and simple life. I always knew that the ladies would be wearing one of three dresses, and that it would be covered with a well-worn apron.

> There is no greater loan than a sympathetic ear.
>
> —FRANK TYGER

During each visit, Vance would share all of her aches and pains. I always had a good knowledge of her medical problems by the time I left. On the other hand, Eileen was always chipper and never complained. If she had a problem, it was always getting better. (You can probably guess who my favorite sister was.)

An old gas stove in the middle of the living room heated the home, and while we sat around it in the winters, the sisters would share stories of earlier days when a wood stove sat there instead. The house had been passed along from their mother after her death. (The father had left the home early when the girls were still young.) Most of our conversations during our visits dealt with the sisters' early childhood years, their humble beginnings, and a mother who loved and provided for their safety and needs.

The ladies spoke of their mother's interest in helping people who worked in the nursing profession. For several years, the ladies talked of recognizing their mother by starting a scholarship fund. They were very deliberative and slow about the prospect of starting a fund, but, after a period of time, they considered me their friend and someone they could trust.

> It's nice to be important, but it's more important to be nice.
>
> —ANONYMOUS

I will never forget the day when they finally decided that a scholarship fund would be the best way to remember their mother. I had suggested that we place a picture of their mother in the nursing department of our university. I did not realize that the picture on the wall was the only picture they had of their mother. As I removed it from the wall I assured them that I would get a copy made yet that day and return the picture. I realized at that moment their trust. They were entrusting me with a family heirloom that was their only tangible reminder of their mother. Needless to say, I was very careful to get the photograph reproduced and returned that very day.

In the fall of 1998, Vance came down with a cold, which later turned into pneumonia, and she ended up in the hospital. Eileen made many trips on her own and, on occasion, I would take her to the hospital. I visited Vance nearly every day myself. Each day, Vance's health continued to decline, and her breathing became more difficult. Both Eileen and I spent the night with Vance at the hospital as she struggled for her life.

> Donors don't give to institutions. They invest in ideas and people in whom they believe.
>
> —G.T. SMITH

Finally, Vance passed away, and a very lonely Eileen returned to an empty home. I knew that we would need to find someone to stay with Eileen, because she was fearful of staying alone. In fact, for several weeks we found a lady who slept downstairs with Eileen. On one occasion, when I was unable to find Eileen at home, I proceeded to the cemetery where I found Eileen lying on her sister's grave talking to her sister. For a time I simply observed her. Then, I went to Eileen's side to give her reassurance that her sister was in a better place and that she knew how much Eileen loved her.

About a year later, after making several visits to Eileen's home and after securing a number of ladies to stay with her, I received a call from one of the ladies requesting that I come immediately.

"Eileen has fallen in the kitchen and is unable to get up," the caretaker said.

I drove to the home and found Eileen on the floor. She was in pain as she cried for help, and I knew that we needed an ambulance. After several hours in the emergency room, the doctor determined that Eileen had broken her hip. Eileen spent about two weeks in the hospital before she was transferred to a nursing home. Daily, and sometimes twice a day, I visited Eileen in the nursing home where her condition continued to grow worse.

On April 4, 2000, I received a call from the nursing home stating that Eileen had died.

The Jett Scholarship fund was established in the amount of $1.3 million dollars. Neither Vance nor Eileen was an alumna of our university. They were not even members of The Wesleyan Church. They were not part of any scholarship banquets. They did not receive any recognition for themselves by giving this wonderful gift. They never had a complete tour of campus. But I was their friend, and they were mine. And that simple fact has made careers in nursing possible for countless students.

INVEST YOURSELF, TOO

Each year the university president and I made a trip to Florida to call on "snowbirds," donors who seemed to be more relaxed and charitable in the warmer climate. In the early years we did not have money to fly, so we scheduled a trip driving through Ohio, Tennessee, Kentucky, North Carolina, Georgia, and finally arrived in Florida. In an attempt to be good stewards of our time, I generally scheduled seven to 10 visits a day. That was great for the first couple of nights, but after a week with that schedule and crashing in donors' homes, we began to feel like zombies.

The nights were always quite an experience for both the president and for me. Since I snore, he always came equipped with a set of earplugs. Invariably, the bedroom would have two twin beds, about two to three feet apart. For us, luxury was two separate rooms. Needless to say, as the night progressed I would hear the famous snap of the president's finger telling me, "Munday, turn over." My snoring was overpowering his earplugs. I recall nights when the president gave up on me and took his blanket and moved to the bathtub. That worked until someone needed to use the bathroom. Other nights I might discover that he had moved to the backseat of the car to sleep.

By the end of the trip, we often had sore throats and occasionally would nod off while we were talking with donors. Grace Crowder, who we routinely visited, knew that we would need some medical attention by the time we reached her house. She became known as Doctor Grace.

Some adventures were forgettable, but we never forgot a dinner one evening in Madison, Florida. This was the first time we had visited our hostess, and she had insisted that we have dinner with her. When we arrived she was busy preparing the meal. We looked around the kitchen to see her large, long-haired cat jump up and meander across the table. I caught the president's eye as he followed the cat. He was allergic to most animals, so I knew that we were in deep trouble. At that point, we were invited to join her at the table for dinner. As if the cat wasn't enough, I saw the president fishing a hair out of his soup. It was all I could do to keep my composure. From across the table, the roll of his eyes said it all.

> Getting money is not all a man's business: to cultivate kindness is a valuable part of the business of life.
>
> —SAMUEL JOHNSON

Next came the main course. As I turned over my napkin, I saw a lip-shaped smear of tomato paste on the backside of the napkin. I couldn't resist showing the president my napkin from under the table. It was all that either of us could do to keep a straight face — and to keep eating.

Each year one of our faithful donors, a former prisoner of war, Tom Stone, invited Ross Hoffman and me to join him on a fishing trip to Isle Royale, located in Lake Superior. The fishing trip involved traveling to Houghton, Michigan, catching a ferryboat, and then traveling for six hours to reach the remote island. On this particular trip I took both of my sons as well as my colleague, Ross.

About two hours into fishing the first day, the fish began to hit in the harbor, and we sprang into action. All of a sudden, I saw a hook with a long, dangling lure coming right at me. I ducked as quickly as I could, but my reflexes proved insufficient. The hook went through my right ear. The boys and Ross both thought it was pretty funny seeing me with a six-inch lure hanging from my ear. I just thought it hurt. We had two options: go to the hospital and have the barb cut off and probably waste the rest of the day of fishing, or pull the hook out ourselves and continue fishing. Tom asked Ross to take over steering the boat and took out a pair of needle nose pliers. Tom gave a huge yank, and I dropped to my knees. My face turned a new shade of white as I kneeled on the floor of the boat trying to regain my composure. Once my boys saw that the hook was free, laughter once again erupted.

Fundraising creates great memories, although all aren't so great at the time. Sometimes we have to "take one for the team" in our line of work. Our work is an investment, and it is well worth it.

That has been apparent in my relationship with Paul and Meredith Kindschi. About 10 years ago, after several years of their giving, I received a telephone call from the couple. I assumed they wanted to arrange a dinner during our next trip to Florida since my wife and I had eaten dinner with them several times at their home in West Palm Beach. But this was a different type call. Paul and Meridith had taken a trip in their Holiday Rambler to Iowa and on their way back home had stopped in Lenoir, North Carolina. Camping had gotten to be too much for them, and they wanted to know if Linda and I would be willing to fly to Charlotte to rescue them and drive them back to Florida. They were ready to get out of the camping activity, an activity that they so long had enjoyed. Paul was eager to show me how to pull the 38-foot camper out of the parking spot as the ladies headed to the front entrance to meet us. As Paul moved the camper forward, the doors of the kitchen cabinets opened and glass dishes came crashing onto the camper floor. It was apparent why we had received the call.

Upon arrival at their home in West Palm, they decided that we should take the Holiday Rambler back to Marion and sell it with the proceeds going to benefit the university. It was a sad day as we carried load after load of items that had been collected over the years in their camping experiences. Now their camping experiences were ending, along with that chapter of their lives. But they were wise enough to recognize when that time came, and I thank God that they called us on that day. I'm honored to be the one they called when they were in need.

As requested, we returned to Marion. Within two weeks, we had sold the motor coach for $54,000. Soon after, they began a scholarship fund. But as time passed, another chapter of their lives passed as well. I received a call from them saying that they were moving to an assisted living apartment, no longer able to live unassisted. They had sold their house and wanted to pay their tithe on it by adding to the scholarship fund. The scholarship fund has reached nearly $300,000, and we regularly speak with the couple about the scholarship's recipients.

Paul, who is now 95 years old, enjoys our visits and, because of his past fundraising experience with the Billy Graham association, always wants to know how we are doing. He has become a great coach and advisor.

Our relationship started more than 20 years ago when a novice fundraiser asked for $25,000 during our first capital campaign, and Paul and Meridith made a gift of $30,000. Right off, he was teaching me; I *should* ask for more! I don't recall ever making that mistake again during my fundraising career. This couple has truly enhanced my life as well as my wife's.

About a month ago, I received a call from Meridith saying that Paul wanted to finish his estate planning to include IWU in his final trust, and asked if I would come to Grand Rapids where they now live. Obviously, I made the trip because of this couple's willingness to be a source of encouragement and strength to me over the years. More than their gifts, their warmth and willingness to share their hearts with us continue to inspire our efforts.

USE YOUR ABILITIES TO THE FULLEST

I have often been cautioned and/or criticized for doing consulting work without charging a fee. My critics generally say the people or institutions that I help will not take me seriously unless I charge them. While this advice has some truth to it, I believe that God rewards our willingness to help others in need. He rejoices in giving, and so should we. In fact, I am currently assisting a Christian school in Marion, motivated, at least in part, by the fact that my grandchildren attend the school. I realize that even with some help the school will struggle financially, and that its nearly 300 stu-

> Always do right.
> This will gratify
> some people, and
> astonish the rest.
>
> —MARK TWAIN

dents will have less of an opportunity to receive a Christian education. **Do I need to turn a profit to enjoy the benefits of the work? Of course not.** We must look at the long-term impact that we are having on the Kingdom. That is the ultimate reward of our work. As Henry A. Rosso, a legendary fundraiser, once said, "Fundraising is not a right — it is a privilege, and we must always honor it as such."

A few years back, a Christian school hired a development director to help pull the school out of its financial troubles. Yet, even after much time, the school continued with a $40,000 to $100,000 deficit. Not only was the fundraiser not raising enough funds for the school, he was not even raising enough money to pay his own salary.

This is the point where I entered the school's picture. The board and principal asked if I would spend a day working with the development director to demonstrate the necessary skills to make an ask and to success-

> True charity is the
> desire to be useful
> to others without
> thought of
> recompense.
>
> —EMANUEL SWEDENBORG

fully raise funds. I was glad to help the school, and immediately accepted the project. I found that his primary challenge was getting too wrapped up in the daily activities of the school. This is true for many fundraisers. With all of the meetings and other obligations, it is easy to lose focus on the process for which you are hired. Sometimes you just have to say 'no' to the meetings, and get out of the office to make donor requests. In this particular case we determined that we would establish a Century Club and ask all donors for $100. God's help was apparent that day as we made 10 calls and received a positive response from each. Our 11th ask was to a gentleman who said he didn't want to join our

Century Club. What he wanted to do was give us $500. In three hours we had raised $1,500 for the school. How I wish we were always so fruitful.

On other occasions I have been able to involve my friends and renowned associates, such as John Maxwell, Jerry Lucas, Clark Kellogg, and Stan Toler in my work with outside schools and organizations. I have put others, myself, and all of our reputations on the line for causes worth believing in. I have executed capital campaigns, seminars, and other events to help promote organizations in need. In some cases, I have spent months or even years with struggling organizations or schools, investing more of my time than I ever expected when I volunteered to help. But, the effort has proven to be rewarding.

Consulting with outside institutions has proven to be one of the most rewarding facets of my career. I have been able to truly impact so many institutions. As fundraisers we must understand that, although we are in competition for dollars with other institutions, we do not necessarily deserve the money more than others. As Christians, we are all in this together. And working together is the only way that we can bring Heaven to earth.

KEY TAKEAWAYS:

- When we make personal investments in our potential donors, we show that we care about them, and not just their money. When people feel cared for, they are more likely to feel comfortable giving.
- As fundraisers, we must understand that although we are in competition for dollars with other institutions, we do not necessarily deserve the money more than others. We must work together if we are going to truly affect God's Kingdom.

PART 4

GOD IS

INTO MORE *THAN*

FUNDS

WE ARE THE BIBLES THE WORLD
IS READING; WE ARE THE CREEDS
THE WORLD IS NEEDING; WE ARE THE
SERMONS THE WORLD IS HEEDING.

—BILLY GRAHAM

CHAPTER 1

∞

SERVING

YOUR DONORS

IN THIS CHAPTER
- Helping donors meet their needs
- A relationship shouldn't — and won't — always be a means to an end

THEIR NEEDS MATTER, TOO

Lonely people do strange things. Luella Hall, a single lady in her 70s, yearned for company so badly that she would make loans — and rent homes — to people who she knew would not pay her back. That required her to make frequent visits to her tenants. She also asked her borrowers to make all payments in person on a monthly basis. These business visits were the primary interactions she had with others.

Decades earlier, Luella had attended IWU for a year and was fond of the university. I made it a priority to visit Luella at her home. We would

Only a life lived
for others is a life
worthwhile.

—ALBERT EINSTEIN

sit around talking about her church. It was the focus of her life and, thus, of our discussions. Much of our time was spent reviewing bad loans she had made and discussing ways I could help her recover the money. During all of my long trips, I would dedicate one or two days attempting to get her books up to date and driving to each of her rentals to collect delinquent rent. It wasn't glamorous, but it was much needed in her life. Her diabetes and blindness during her last five years made it even more difficult for her to collect money people owed her. Eventually, there was no other option, and I told her that I would not continue to help unless she stopped putting herself in positions where others took advantage of her. Fortunately, she consented to my ultimatum after realizing that I was concerned about her welfare. I continued to visit her two to three times each year, and when I was in the area I would stop to see how she was doing. Our staff saw that she was taken care of financially by setting up annuities that supplied her with life income to provide for her monthly needs.

In addition to meeting her daily needs, we worked to help Luella preserve money to establish a scholarship fund in her father's honor. Before her death, we were able to read letters of gratitude to her written by scholarship recipients. And upon her death, she was able to give $250,000 to grow the established fund that would help students pursue a degree in Christian ministries, honoring her father who had served as a minister. We were able to do this because during her life we had protected her finances and cared for her wellbeing.

Donors need to know that you care about them and their situation before they can consider giving to your organization. In a personal survey of the Council for Christian Colleges and Universities, we confirmed that one of the best ways to serve potential donors is through personal visits. **Money is, in fact, very personal.** And you need to treat donors' money as such.

But, there's no one-size-fits-all way to serve donors. Since most people have plenty of needs in their lives, you will have more than enough opportunities to use your strengths to give them a hand. This is most definitely true with my experience with one Indiana Wesleyan University donor and true gentleman, Jim Sutter.

Jim is a Marion High School and Indiana University graduate. He had honored his former high school orchestra teacher, Lloyd DaCosta Jones, with a scholarship fund that has since provided scholarships of $8,000 to $10,000 each year to local students seeking to further their music education — specifically with string instruments.

Jim and his wife, Nedra, have a passion for good music, especially if it is instrumental. They attend many concerts presented by our University Chorale and wind ensembles as well as by the Marion Philharmonic Orchestra, which perform regularly at our university's Phillippe Performing Arts Center. Jim and his brother, Jack, had taken violin lessons under Mr. Jones. Jim indicated that he and Jack were not super players, but the instruction and the instructor's heart for music kept them interested. Because of our need for scholarships in instrumental music, Jim's offer to provide such a scholarship was music to my ears. (No pun intended.) As discussed earlier, anytime you can match a need with a donor's interest you have a win-win situation. Since this was to aid local students, it was a win-win-win.

My relationship with Jim quickly went from professional to personal. Since Jim's family members recognized our friendship, they asked if I would help pull off a surprise party for Jim's 69th birthday celebration. They figured he would expect a 70th party and opted for the earlier birthday instead.

> How wonderful it is that nobody need wait a single moment before starting to improve the world.
>
> —ANNE FRANK

I set the stage by telling Jim that we had invited the daughter of his former music teacher to an IWU reception, even though in reality, the family had prepared an evening of reflection and tribute to Jim. When Jim walked into Baldwin Center on our campus, he was greeted by cheers of over 100 friends and family who had come to celebrate his birthday. After the meal, the group moved to the

Globe Theater across the hall for the roast and exchange of both kind words and candor from the past. Many friends had traveled many miles to have the opportunity to show their love and appreciation for him. Under a banner that read "HAPPY 69th BIRTHDAY!" we watched a video that Jim's son had created in his honor. Jim's smile was priceless as he spoke of his friends and family, and his deep love for them.

Shortly after this party, Jim came to my retirement party on campus and motioned for me to follow him back to my office. There, he grabbed my arm and began forcing a watch on my arm, right next to my Timex. The watch was a Rolex, and I immediately began to refuse the gift as Jim made room on my arm for the new watch. Jim said that the watch was in appreciation for how I had impacted his and Nedra's lives. By this time, tears were flowing from both Jim's and my eyes. To gain composure, Jim left my office by the back door, as other guests entered the front doors to enjoy punch and cookies.

Shortly after my retirement, Jim called to ask if I would meet with him and the executive director of the local YMCA to discuss fundraising. The YMCA had been in an extended effort (several years, in fact) to raise enough money to build a new YMCA. Jim's father had served on the YMCA Board for 35 years, and Jim had served on the Boys' and Girls' Club board for 25 years. The YMCA needed $4 million to complete the project.

Their purpose in visiting my office was to see if I would assist in the fundraising effort. The building would house all of the sports-related venues, including a pool, gym, fitness area, and space for community activities. The plan included remodeling the old Veterans' Memorial Coliseum, which had served as home of the community's annual Easter pageant since World War II, and the home to Marion Giants basketball from 1928 to 1970. Jim was eager to provide the community with a much-needed building without encumbering any debt. Since Jim had such a heart for the project, and because of our friendship, I agreed to help.

During one of our first fundraising calls, we were able to secure a naming opportunity and gift of $500,000. We immediately knew that we had made a good decision to help the YMCA.

After that commitment, while visiting Jim at his home where he was scrambling through the building plans, Jim said that we had to get this building completed without strapping the YMCA with debt.

He looked up from his pages of plans and said, "Terry, I am prepared to give up to $1.75 million to see the project completed."

I then knew just how important the project was to him. It had to succeed, and so I dedicated myself with new resolve to helping the YMCA campaign continue.

In the end, we were able to see Jim's dream turn into a reality. I had the privilege to tour the new YMCA facility as Jim showed me every space that was going to be available to the young people in our community.

But, what made my efforts worthwhile was not the credit he afforded me in helping raise the money, but his heart, his joy, and the commitment he demonstrated in seeing the project brought to a successful completion.

> Kindness in words creates confidence.
> Kindness in thinking creates profundity.
> Kindess in giving creates love.
>
> —LAO-TSE

The new facility preserved memories for thousands of people who had cheered basketball teams in the large basketball arena, and who had observed the solemnity of the Easter pageant. I doubt that there are any people in Marion or Grant County who have not been inside the facility. If there are, Jim is bound to find them and take them on a tour. The membership at the YMCA has doubled since the completion of the new building. They are reaching out to and serving the community in a wonderful way.

This past year, I had the privilege of hearing Jim speak at a Christian businessmen's prayer breakfast. Several minutes into his speech, he looked to the back of the room where I was seated and shared one of the nicest compliments I have ever received.

"This man taught me how to give and has nurtured my spiritual development. I wouldn't be here today without his influence in my life," Jim said.

A RELATIONSHIP ISN'T ALWAYS
A MEANS TO AN END

I once tried — and failed — to cultivate a gift with a gentleman in Florida. But the return on our relationship was as God had intended. The man was about 45 years old at the time and had hardly ever held a job. Still, he was rich. He was the product of a wealthy family, and he was equally eccentric. During one of our frequent visits, I noticed that in his garage he had stored about eight fishing poles — all exactly the same. He liked a particular fishing rod and reel, so he bought several in case that model was discontinued. On another visit, I saw construction workers removing the insulation from his new home. He had read an article that indicated that cellulose in the attic was bad for your health. Another time, the construction workers were removing the countertops from his kitchen, not because they were worn or had spots on them, but because the same look in the kitchen for more than four or five years made him feel depressed. Each visit brought new issues. He was always trying a new diet, such as ground vegetables, to improve his health. The food substances were nasty to see, let alone to consume, and with each visit I noticed that he was becoming more frail and appeared to be undernourished. On several occasions we would stand around the piano and sing old hymns. He had a sincere interest in music and had a wide assortment of electronic music equipment that could have rivaled a small orchestra.

> For everyone to whom much is given, from him much will be required; and to whom much has been committed, of him they will ask the more.
>
> —LUKE 12:48

Then I received word that he had placed a $1 million gift in his local church offering plate, although we had never been able to secure a gift from him. Still, we maintained a strong relationship, which by many, may seem just plain odd — or even stupid. Although there is a limit to the amount of time a fundraiser can spend in seeking donors or a donation, it is difficult to resign your pursuit of a prospect until it becomes clear that you have been fully written off. In this case, the gentleman later renounced his belief in Christ and wanted to have nothing to do with Christianity. At that point I realized that it would be difficult to either minister or receive a gift for the university. After a couple more visits, when he failed to answer the door, I knew my effectiveness with him was in question.

As humans, we never can direct potential donors' desires and actions. All we can ever hope to do is present a true picture of our mission, and in turn, encourage Christ-like generosity. We must also accept that our relationships with potential donors will often not yield the results for which we have hoped.

But even if such relationships do not end in a check, they can end in the furthering of God's will. **If we understand that our relationships with others give us the opportunity to serve others and make life a bit more pleasant for those we encounter, no meeting, visit, or phone call can ever be a waste.** Likewise, it's important to maintain a relationship with people after they have given generously to your cause, even if you do not expect, or want, to raise any more money from them.

For example, I have an elderly couple who have given IWU almost all of their estate. In the case of the gentleman, Ken Bostic is suffering from dementia and is not able to carry on a conversation as he has in the past. I know the questions he will ask me each time I visit. "How are you today?" and "What is new in your life?" Beyond those questions, he is at a loss for words. Yet I visit him at least once each week and sometimes more. I pick him up for church when he is able, and during Sunday school I fix him his favorite hot drink, hot chocolate. I pay his bills, deposit his checks and do other chores because we have developed a friendship over the years, and he has been very kind to the organization that I represent. We take rides in the car and sing verses of some of the old hymns together.

Why? Because he enjoys that fellowship; and I enjoy bringing some joy and quality to his life.

Such personal relationships with donors are often just as much a blessing to our lives as they are to the donors' lives. My relationship with Ken began 15 years ago after I visited him on his farm. Because of my childhood days of farming, we immediately hit it off. We worked together around his farm on projects such as putting new siding on his barn. After he had suffered a heart attack and received a pacemaker, his farming days were over, but he wanted to make Marion his home to be near his friends and the university. After having lived in the university-owned assisted living for the past three years, I am confident Ken believes he made the right decision. Love surrounds him there. Recently, my wife and I took Ken and his wife, Marceil, on a four-hour round trip back to their home church to visit people they had worshiped with for more than 60 years.

Ken and Marceil were content to return to Marion. After our long day, Ken turned to me and said, "Thanks for doing that for us. We appreciate you." We just recently celebrated his 94th birthday, and I am thankful for each of those years I have been able to be part of his life. Needless to say, my friendship goes beyond the money that he has given and beyond the meaningful conversations that we once had. It is rooted in our hearts. Through my work, God has blessed us both with wonderful friends.

KEY TAKEAWAYS:

- Relationships with potential donors can be blessings to you and the donor, providing friendships that will last a lifetime.
- There's no one-size-fits-all way to serve donors because no two donors are the same. Luella Hall's needs were much different than Ken Bostic's needs, and we responded to them accordingly.
- As Christian fundraisers, we must teach donors to give, nurturing their spiritual development along the way.

CHAPTER 2

EXPANDING GOD'S KINGDOM

IN THIS CHAPTER
- Promoting God's work through financial support
- The most important service is salvation

We raise awareness, involvement, and dollars. But if those objectives don't lead to the advancement of God's Kingdom, we have failed as Christians and as fundraisers. This is, indeed, our ultimate goal, and we must always keep it uppermost in our minds and hearts.

Working for Christian organizations automatically steers us in that direction. At Indiana Wesleyan University, for example, the advancement team has raised tens of millions of dollars to benefit our students. Those funds have allowed us to prepare students who have served as pastors,

> God's work is not man working for God; it is God's own work; through often wrought
>
> —HUDSON TAYLOR

counselors and missionaries—all of them spreading His good news throughout the world. Our fundraising, although directly for the university, is actually for God's greater mission. The university is one more conduit for His ultimate goal.

As John Haggai writes in *Paul J. Meyer and the Art of Giving*, fundraisers must act as "stalwart modern philanthropists who synchronize their priorities with the express command of God in Scripture, who march to the divine drumbeat. They [must] impact the world — yes, the world — for God."[1] And although we surely fulfill that goal, many times we do not see the effects of our efforts directly. We cannot touch, hold, or feel them. We have to believe.

SERVING HIS MISSION

Fortunately for our morale, every now and again, we have the blessing of seeing the direct effects of our work. That's exactly what happened when I put my money and reputation on the line for Indiana Wesleyan's students. I saw God's plan unfold.

During my first years as vice president for advancement at IWU, students often came to my office in search of funds to continue and complete their educations. Often the visitors were international students who had saved enough money to make it to the States, but after a year or so found their campus accounts almost drained.

One such student came to me, ready, yet reluctant, to return home to Canada without finishing her degree. Her father was sitting in the van, with an attached trailer loaded with his daughter's belongings. He could not afford to pay her IWU tuition any longer.

The exchange rate between Canada and the United States had recently shifted to the detriment of the student. The $10,000 tuition bill in U.S. dollars translated to $14,000 in Canadian currency, a figure that was far outside her family's financial capability.

After some discussion with the student, I learned that she was an excellent singer. That gave me an idea.

The university's Church Relations Office coordinates several vocal teams that travel throughout the country. Students who participate in the teams earn nearly $4,000 — a perfect opportunity for this young woman to continue her education — at IWU. Together, the two of us presented the idea to her father. After many tears, and even more persuasion, he agreed to the proposal.

As we had hoped, her membership with the Christian ministry team provided the means for her to pay her tuition bill in full. Not only was she able to continue her Christian education, but she also enriched the campus community through her talent. It was a blessing to both her and the university — and a beautiful manifestation of God's work.

> The kingdom of God does not come with your careful observation, nor will people say, "Here it is," or "There it is," because the kingdom of God is among you.
>
> —LUKE 17:20–21

Another foreign student by the name of Job Towett frequently visited my office for financial assistance. The young man from Kenya often found himself shy on money for small, day-to-day items: books, shoes, and the like. When he entered my office, he was not asking for a handout. He asked if I had any work for him to do, so that he could give before receiving. Fortunately, at least for Job, I buy, remodel, and sell houses, so I was able to keep him busy with odd jobs. Most importantly, I was able to keep him from passively accepting charity — a great concern for both of us.

By the end of Job's junior year, however, odd jobs just weren't enough. The business office had adopted a new policy that required students to have a fully paid account before registering for their senior year. Job's account had a $3,400 balance, and there was not enough time to raise that much money before registration. After exploring several options, I borrowed the $3,400 from the bank and paid off his account myself.

As Job sat at my family's kitchen table the following Thanksgiving (international students could often not return home over the short break, and my wife and I welcomed them into our home), he told us that he wanted to name his future children after us. If the child were a boy, it would be named Terry, and if it were a girl, the name would be Linda. He so appreciated our hospitality. Allowing these students to complete their educations was a thrill that only eternity can match.

For good reason, members of the administrative council began to tease me for my soft touch with students. Stories of these students spread across campus, and I was quickly becoming the man to see if you couldn't pay your tuition bill. But I was glad to take on the role. I knew from my own experience that a strong Christian education was life changing. I could not bear the thought of the university denying any student his or her full education.

> Pray as if everything depended upon God and work as if everything depended upon man.
>
> —FRANCIS CARDINAL SPELLMAN

In due time, an American student who also had a hefty balance going into his senior year came to me for help. Elliot Miller had a balance of $7,700, and it appeared he would have to drop out of school for a year to work, and then return to finish his degree in elementary education. As the young man sat in my office, we prayed that God would provide the finances necessary to complete his schooling. Christ was our hope.

After Elliot left my office, I honestly didn't give much more thought to his situation or to our prayer. But my memory — and interest — was jogged about a week later when I received a call from a woman in Ohio who was interested in starting a scholarship fund for a male elementary school teacher. *Could this be Elliot's chance?* I asked myself.

The woman wanted to encourage more men to become elementary school teachers because one of her daughter's best educational experiences came in the classroom of a male teacher. Because of my previous experience in education, I knew that male elementary school teachers could be great role models for both boys and girls.

As we talked, the woman said she wanted to donate about 285 shares of Eagle Picher stock to get the scholarship fund started. "How much is the stock selling for today?" I asked.

"About $27 a share," she said.

By that time I had my desk drawer open and plugged the numbers into my calculator. The total that appeared on the calculator screen was just about $7,700. *This is the answer to Elliot's and my prayer,* I thought. And I didn't want the opportunity to pass Elliot by.

"May I tell you about one of our male elementary education majors who's currently in financial need?" I asked.

"Of course," she said.

As I proceeded to tell her about this young man, she decided that establishing a scholarship fund could wait. Elliot needed the money right then.

After graduating from Indiana Wesleyan the next year, Elliot took a job as a fourth-grade teacher in the Marion schools, and married his college sweetheart, Melody, who also taught elementary classes. At home, the two didn't seem to have opportunities to share God's work as they had so eagerly hoped. Either they could teach at Christian schools, where the students already had Christian backgrounds, or they could teach in public schools where presenting the gospel was more challenging. Elliot and Melody continued to look for teaching jobs where they could help fulfill the Great Commission.

They first found that opportunity at Hephzibah Children's Home, which is located in Macon, Georgia. After teaching there for a few years, the Millers picked up and moved again — this time to China. They were seizing a blessed opportunity to work together for the country's International Schools, which support a strong Christian curriculum. The six International Schools of China impact more than 1,000 children from around the world, from kindergarten through 12th grade. Most of the students — be they Korean, Malaysian, Filipino, or European — have never heard the gospel. Elliot, their principal, and Melody, their teacher, now make sure they do.

Although nearly two decades would pass before we were aware of the full impact of the money on Elliot's life, it took only the change of a few seasons for us to receive the first sign of good faith. Less than a year after the stock was sold to help finance Elliott's education, Eagle Picher products were found to contain asbestos contaminants. The company almost immediately declared bankruptcy, and its stock hit rock bottom. Without God's providence, those 285 shares would have been worthless.

This incident confirmed to the donor and to me that she had followed God's admonition by making the gift. She had assisted a young man who in turn has helped, and continues to help, others around the world. And it all started with a small prayer in my office and an unexpected telephone call from a woman in Ohio who I had never met.

DEMONSTRATING CHRIST'S LOVE TO DONORS

Non-Christians can serve as great donors to Christian organizations, as we proved earlier with Adam Ray's donation of $3.5 million. But, reaching out to such donors is not only beneficial in a financial sense. Doing so can help build bridges to so much more.

After several months of working with Adam, we became friends. And as his friend, I not only searched for ways for IWU to benefit from our relationship, but I also tried to serve Adam the best that I could. I so wanted to show him how much God loved him, but my manifestations were always limited to the urbane.

> As soon as a man has found Christ, he begins to find others.
>
> —CHARLES SPURGEON

Adam's home was the most visible source of need in his life, so I decided to start there. I had long worked on renovating homes as a side job, so I took on the task of assisting Adam with some changes to his home. Although reluctant at first to accept my offer, he eventually consented to let me work on a few projects. The roof was replaced to protect the already stained and peeling walls that showed several years of damage. And after convincing Adam that I knew a man who could complete drywall work for only $100, Adam told me to proceed. He didn't want me spending money on his home. Adam's close friend and life partner, Debbie, who he had recently married, tried to give me money for materials used in each repair, but I always replied, "No thanks." After all the couple had done for the school, I wanted to do something just for them.

It was during this time that Adam called to say he was planning to have a hernia operation. He wanted me to know, but assured me that it would be an outpatient procedure — a one-night stay maximum. I offered to join him and Debbie at the hospital, but he insisted that it wasn't necessary.

A couple of days later, Debbie called, and I could sense from her quivering voice that she was worried. Adam was undergoing further tests. I immediately went to the hospital where I found Adam emotionally drained from his procedures — and the stress of the unknown. Together, we waited for the test results.

The doctors found that Adam had a malignant tumor on his lung and they expected that he had only two to three months to live. That December, the hospital became his new and final home. The staff at Indiana Wesleyan, under the direction of Sally Cramer, decided to bring some Christmas spirit to him by placing a small Christmas tree in his room. The staff placed 21 presents beneath its branches — one for each of the 21 days leading up to Christmas. The first gift was a disposable camera. And we all started capturing the festivities. Each day as Adam opened his gift, he insisted that one of his visitors be in each of his pictures.

> A man can eat his dinner without understanding exactly how food nourishes him. A man can accept what Christ has done without knowing how it works: indeed, he certainly would not know how it works until he has accepted it.
>
> —C.S. LEWIS

Adam and Debbie had no children, so I knew the importance of a daily visit to the hospital. Almost every day I arrived at the hospital by 7:30 a.m. and remained for at least an hour and a half. My secretary, Lisa Poole, always knew where I was in the mornings. Some days called for several visits, others called for a hand to hold during chemotherapy treatments. After several weeks of this routine, Adam's health began to decline. The end was apparent, and it struck me that Adam could leave this world without knowing or accepting Christ as his personal Savior. **He could give IWU all of his money, but if in the end he did not know Christ's love, I would have failed him.** I would have failed him as a Christian and as a friend.

One Sunday morning in January of 2001, on my way to church, I stopped by the hospital as I did most Sundays. On this particular day, I sensed a need for a different kind of visit. I told Adam that although I had prayed many times for his cancer, I wanted to pray for his heart condition: his salvation. He said that would be okay, and I told him that he could join in or repeat the prayer that I said. It was the sinner's prayer, the simple yet eternally powerful words that all who are Christians have prayed to receive Christ as their personal Savior:

> Heavenly Father, I know that I have sinned against you and that my sins separate me from you. I am truly sorry. I now want to turn away from my past sinful life and turn to you for forgiveness. Please forgive me, and help me avoid sinning again. I believe that your son, Jesus Christ, died for my sins, was resurrected from the dead, is alive, and hears my prayer. I invite Jesus to become the Lord of my life, to rule and reign in my heart from this day forward. Please send your Holy Spirit to help me obey You, and to do Your will for the rest of my life. In Jesus' name I pray, Amen.[2]

Adam whispered the words after me. His heart sang them to Heaven. When we had closed the prayer, I opened my eyes and Adam stood up with tears coursing down his cheeks. He embraced me by wrapping his thinning arms around my body. Debbie, not accustomed to this kind of emotional display by Adam, moved quickly to the back of Adam to gather the backside of his revealing hospital gown.

He accepted Christ as his personal Savior that day in his hospital room. About a week later, Adam asked me if he should be baptized. I explained to him that baptism was a symbol of his repentance of sins and faith in

Christ. He firmly replied, "I want to be baptized then." I called on a friend, Reverend Andy Schramm, from the Westminster Presbyterian Church, to perform the ceremony. The Reverend made his way to the hospital the next morning where he was joined by 15 to 20 members of the Indiana Wesleyan advancement staff for the baptism ceremony. Little did we suspect that Debbie, who had been present when Adam yielded his heart to Christ, would ask Reverend Schramm if he would baptize her as well.

> God's gift put man's best dreams to shame.
>
> —ELIZABETH BARRETT BROWNING

When I met Adam, I was interested in what he could do for IWU. Later, my concern shifted to what I could do for him; and it took Adam's illness to remind me of that importance. The most significant element in our relationship was what God could do for Adam through me. And He proved that by helping me turn both Adam and Debbie's hearts to Him.

What a glorious sight there in that hospital room — a husband and wife, 77 and 78 years of age, receiving the sacrament of baptism. I keep that memory dear to my heart each time I meet non-Christian potential donors. As Christians, we have a responsibility to demonstrate God's love to all those we encounter — even if we are asking them for money. We can expand His Kingdom in ways we simply never foresee.

KEY TAKEAWAYS:

- If our work doesn't lead to the advancement of God's Kingdom, we have failed as Christians and as fundraisers. God's Kingdom should always be our ultimate goal.
- IWU received $3.5 million from Adam and Debbie Ray. But, I am so much happier for the personal growth and ultimate salvation that we helped to secure in their lives. A soul means so much more than money.

TERRY MUNDAY

Terry Munday served for 18 years as Vice President for University Advancement at Indiana Wesleyan University in Marion, Indiana, where he received a bachelor's degree in 1970.

Indiana Wesleyan, during Munday's two decades as its chief fund-raiser, rose from the brink of bankruptcy to become one of America's fastest-growing Christian universities with enrollment now exceeding 15,000 students.

Munday, who has bachelor's, master's and specialist in education degrees, went from teaching to serve 14 years as a public school administrator—including eight years as a superintendent.

Munday has written a book about his self-taught-but-always-creative experiences as a professional fund-raiser. While semi-retired from Indiana Wesleyan, he continues to serve as a consultant to the university and to other Christian non-profit organizations around the country.

Munday and his wife Linda, who both are Ohio natives, have been married for 42 years. They continue to live in Marion, Indiana, to be near their four children and seven grandchildren.

NOTES

PART 1
CHAPTER 1

1. Howard Dayton, *Your Money Counts* (Wheaton, Illinois: Tyndale House, 1997), 1-2.
2. Alan Gotthardt, *The Eternity Portfolio* (Wheaton, Illinois: Tyndale House, 2003), 73.
3. Rob Moll, "Scrooge Lives!" http://www.christianitytoday.com/ct/2008/december/10.24.html.
4. Joel Betz, "Shame on Us," *World Magazine*, August 24, 2002, http://www.world mag.com/ articles/6247.

CHAPTER 2

1. Alan Gotthardt, *The Eternity Portfolio* (Wheaton, Illinois: Tyndale House, 2003), 86.
2. GivingUSA, GivingUSA Foundation Press Releases http://www.givingusa.org/press_releases/gusa.cfm
3. Harris Interactive DonorPulse, "While a Third of Adults Think the Nonprofit Sector in the United States is Headed in the Wrong Direction, a Vast Majority of Households have Donated to Charities in the Past Year," http://www.harrisinteractive.com/harris_poll/index.asp?PID=657
4. Charles Piller and Doug Smith, "For-profit fundraisers collect loads, but nonprofits see a sliver," *Los Angeles Times*, July 06, 2008, http://articles.latimes.com/ 2008/ju/06/local/me-charity6?pg=1.
5. Ibid.
6. GivingUSA, GivingUSA Foundation Press Releases http://www.givingusa.org/press_releases/gusa.cfm
7. Randy Alcorn, *Money, Possessions, and Eternity* (Carol Stream, Illinois: Tyndale House, 1989), 39.
8. Dr. Thomas Kinnan, Dissertation, Pastor of BreakPointe Community Church, Overland Park, Kansas, used by permission.

PART 2
CHAPTER 2

1. Randy Alcorn, *The Treasure Principle* (Colorado: Multnomah Publishers, 2001), 29.

PART 4
CHAPTER 2

1. Jon Edmund Haggai, *Paul J. Meyer and the Art of Giving* (Atlanta: Kobrey Press) 1994, 101.
2. Wikipedia, "Sinner's Prayer" http://en.wikipedia.org/Sinner's_prayer#cite_ note-1.